Hurry Up And Wait....

By Edna Blake

Edna Blake
Waiting brings
us into His presence —

First Printing, January 2003

For information contact Edna Blake at:
14 Merribrook Court • O'Fallon, MO • 63366
E-mail: WildSocks@aol.com
636-978-6320
or visit her website at www.EdnaBlake.com

ISBN: 0-9668906-2-0

Scripture quotations, used by permission are from:
The Touchpoint Bible – The New Living Translation 1996

Cover, illustrations and layout by:
Kathy Allen • St. Louis, MO
E-mail: artbykallen@go2netmail.com

Printed in the United States of America.

Sue Adams   Barb Ellis   Mehra Nour

Betty Arnold   Ron Farnum   Tom O'Connor

Nancy Basden   Jackie Forkan   Karel Owens

Linda Beaver   Linda Gaikwaa   Jerry Peters

Marilyn Beckman   Terry Gann   Judy Price

Marilyn Bell   Becky Grimes   Joann Randall

I would like to dedicate this book to all of my friends from the ON TRACK, Singles Ministry. We have been learning the Art of Waiting and are presently being refined by the process.   Joan Rankin

Tim Bennett   Bill Gronemyer   Carolyn Risher

We have been learning how *waiting* is one of God's ways of maturing us in our daily faith walk with Christ. My friends have labored with me again during the time it takes to write a book. They have also loved me, prayed for me and given me positive feed-back. They have graciously allowed me to practice on them...

Karen Benson   Norman Hoffman   Freeda Robinson

Thanks.   Mary Hollis   Jan Shelton

Sharon Berkel   Nina Howard   Susan Skinner

Brenda Birrittier   Bob Hassing   Bonnie Smith

Marsha Bland   Pat Kinne   Jackie Smith

Barb Buchheit   Neil Klocke   Ruth South

Will Caraker   Linda Kuhn   Jeanne Tain

Carol Christensen   Linda Lamar   Chuck Troxel

Jim Cook   Carol Lapinski   Jane Veazey

Becky Couvion   Maxine Lapinski   Nancy Weaver

Mary Cribbin   Mary Lopp   Pat Wilds

Vicky Curry   Pauline Marko   Alan Williams

Barbara Dale   Bob Meyerott   Marilyn Williams

Linda Drummond   Tanner Morrow   Richard Wolfrom

Sharon Duss   Mary Jane Norris   Linda Wood

Pete Elkan

Table of Contents

Journaling Moments

These are brief encounters with life and living...appointments in waiting...hopefully, they will help you reflect upon the waiting process and encourage you to record your waiting times with the Father.

Introduction

Have you ever thought about how many lines you have stood in over the course of your life-time? The time you have spent waiting for some colossal, huge extra ordinary experience to hit you in the face? The frantic rush...the constant and on-going run, run, run, while still trying to deal with all of those little interruptions! Being put on hold...or being told to pick a number. Life for the most part is about taking your turn and waiting in line!

The "Waiting Game," is really about learning how God has a *plan for our lives as well as a purpose!* The refining of silver takes time and the silversmith recognizes the silver is true when he is able to see his reflection in the product. When God can see the reflection of His Son in our lives, He knows the time of waiting has been worth-while. I think we know it too!

I personally think the refining time is taking more time than I am prepared to give. I *Hurry Up And Wait*...it seems to consume my life. I keep wondering if I am learning the significance God intends for me to learn during this time of waiting. It is a precious time...waiting for God to do His complete work in my life, which by the way, this side of eternity is never going to happen.

Waiting for God...is actually ACTION...waiting for God to Act in my life...for His glory.

I have shared with you some of my Journaling Moments which have focused on the waiting times. I am hoping you can identify mine along with yours. I was reminded of God's care and His patience with me during my process. I hope you will be encouraged to remember your process and ask God to reveal more of His character to you as you mature in your faith walk.

This book is designed for you to take notes and to write your own journal...remember your struggles, and as you remember, you can also celebrate the remarkable work of the Holy Spirit and how He is active in your own personal life. You can observe His handy work along the way as you are waiting in the wings!

These little Journaling Moments have been created to give you a time to reflect and ponder your own life segments related to your life experiences. You have an opportunity *now* to write in your own words...the Journaling Moments of your life!

DAY 1

I've been waiting... but nothing is happening!

*Second Wind: We don't have to worry about falling or failing...
if we remember we can fly!*

Do you sometimes think about people who have lost their vision? I am not talking about physical sight...I am talking about their vision! They have lost their enthusiasm for life and living. They worry about the event before it happens! Can you identify with that kind of mind set? Maybe you are guilty of thinking in those terms from time to time... it is subtle!

Isaiah 46:4
"I will be your God throughout your lifetime–until your hair is white with age. I made you, and I will care for you. I will carry you along and save you."

Isaiah 40: 27-31
"O Israel, how can you say the LORD does not see your troubles? How can you say God refuses to hear your case? Have you never heard or understood? Don't you know that the LORD is the everlasting God, the Creator of all the earth? He never grows faint or weary. No one can measure the depths of his understanding. He gives power to those who are tired and worn out; he offers strength to the weak. Even youths will become exhausted, and young men will give up. But those who wait on the LORD will find new strength. They will fly high on wings like eagles. They will run and not grow weary. They will walk and not faint."

Recreational joggers will sometimes experience the phenomenon of a *Second Wind*. They are in the midst of running along at a pretty good pace and then suddenly they come to a place along the way, when they start thinking, "I can't go another block." Then it happens, out of nowhere comes a new surge of energy and they feel strengthened. Serious runners come to expect that burst of energy...they count on it!

11

In Duluth, MN during the Marathon Race, Grandma's Race, the runners would come to what they called, "Lemon Drop Hill". People would be standing along side shouting words of encouragement...they had come a long way, and they were starting to get tired. People would be on the sidelines with water and words of strength. "Keep going, you can do it"...and somehow, at that hill, they were able to pick up the pace and make it to the finish line.

The key for me is learning to wait upon the Lord...waiting for Him to lift me up and to come along side of me during the specific time in my life when I had run out of steam. For me it is my **Second Wind!** He gives power to those who are weak and to those who need strength...He takes over!

The struggles and the hardships are not gone...but they have now become manageable because I am relying upon the source of strength in my life. Jesus! Our family made it through hard times with creative ideas and recipes. Remember God has not forgotten his recipe for Manna. We ate Okra burgers, Hot Dog helper, Goomeegam, Kang Fang, and Must Go Soup. We still enjoy some of those dishes...simply because it reminds us of the hard times and God's faithfulness to us...plus, it's good eating! How crazy is that? God is a creative God in the midst of the periods we think are about waiting...we think nothing is happening, nothing is going on...how foolish! Good chili takes time on the back burner in order to be really good! I sometimes enjoy it even more the second day!

The second half is the most challenging and it is also very exciting! It is our Second Wind!

Romans 12:9-21
"Don't just pretend that you love others. Really love them. Hate what is wrong. Stand on the side of the good. Love each other with genuine affection, and take delight in honoring each other. Never be lazy in your work, but serve the Lord enthusiastically.

Be glad for all God is planning for you. Be patient in trouble, and always be prayerful. When God's children are in need, be the one to help them out. And get into the habit of inviting guests home for diner or, if they need lodging, for the night.

If people persecute you because you are a Christian, don't curse them; pray that God will bless them. When others are happy, be happy with them. If they are sad, share their sorrow. Live in harmony with each other. Don't try to act important, but enjoy the company of ordinary people. And don't think you know it all!

Never pay back evil for evil to anyone. Do things in such a way that everyone can see you are honorable. Do your part to live in peace with everyone as much as possible.

Dear friends, never avenge yourselves. Leave that to God. For it is written, 'I will take vengeance; I will repay those who deserve it,' says the Lord.

Instead, do what the Scriptures say: 'If your enemies are hungry, feed them. If they are thirsty, give them something to drink, and they will be ashamed of what they have done to you.'"

Don't let evil get the best of you, but conquer evil by doing good."

Here it Comes...are you ready...right in our face! The Scripture speaks to us clearly.

> **1 Corinthians 15:58**
> "So, my dear brothers and sisters be strong and steady, always enthusiastic about the Lord's work, for you know that nothing you do for the Lord is ever useless."
>
> **1 Corinthians 16:13**
> "Be on guard. Stand true to what you believe. Be courageous. Be strong. And everything you do must be done with love."

These promises help us to live our lives in the Second Half...in the time of our Second Wind, we are to actually enjoy the season and to be thankful for His faithfulness and His promises. Nothing we do for the Lord is useless...nothing! Everything has value when it is given to Him!

God has the plan but it often takes us some time to figure out the purpose. We question what we are supposed to be learning from this little adventure platform at the Learning Station? How does this fit together in the overall plan God has for our lives. Sometimes I can see God's purpose in the lives of others, but looking at my own plan gets a little confusing.

Trust the Planner...Partner with Him and you will remember how to Fly! My husband was this huge planner...he marked out things for my life that kept me busy for two years after his home-going. Half of the things he planned for me, I would never have even thought about doing...but all of them fit together and because I did each of the items on the list he left for me I was able to sell our house for a better price. He understood the plan and the purpose. I could only understand it after I actually experienced the purpose. When we don't have all of the pieces, we learn the valuable lesson of walking by faith and not by sight!

Galatians 6:9
"Don't get discouraged and give up, for we will reap a harvest of blessing at the appropriate time."

Are you living in the time of your Second Wind? If not, unless the Lord comes or you and I go home to Glory, we will be living in the time of our *Second Wind*! How do you want to fly? My son, Dan, is taking flying lessons and he is so excited about what is happening in his life. He called to tell me about landing and taking off in the plane. Are you excited about where God has you in this moment of time? We don't have to be afraid of the future...the waiting period will be part of the training time...so when we get to that stage...we can have total confidence in the Planner!

How has this Modern Day Parable helped you deal with the Waiting Process? This is an opportunity for you to journal your thoughts and process with God...Give it a try.

My Daily Journal

DAY

1

Timing is everything! Says who?

DAY 2

Timing is everything for the little brown bats, a common species in the Northern United States. Though they mate in the fall, females store sperm to delay birth until June and July, when insects provide a feast for them and their young. A colony of 500 can devour 500,000 mosquito size insects in an hour. *National Geographic...July, 2001*

"Hurry Up And Wait!"...for what? I read this little article while traveling out to see my children in Mesa, AZ. I was thinking about my children and all of our lives. I was realizing how God knows it all...He knows the plan and He knows the purpose. I was challenged and blessed in thinking about how perfect God's plan and purpose is. It was one of those God Moments. *Another time when God gave me a clear picture of His goodness...and a spiritual reality check!*

Ecclesiastes 11:4
"If you wait for perfect conditions, you will never get anything done."

Time waits for no man...or woman. We have to treasure the moments. Time is a gift, while we are waiting for the purpose...we need to live in the present. How do we live in the moment? I used to be concerned about trying to do things perfectly, but as I got older I realized, I couldn't do anything perfectly but I could do my best. I learned I could enjoy those less than perfect moments. I could be OK with not being perfect! How freeing! I have learned to make lemonade out of lemons.

Baking and cooking...if I waited for perfect conditions...*A time when I might have all of the ingredients, or the perfect, no-fail recipe, if I waited, I can tell you I would never have cooked or baked anything!*

But, because I learned to improvise, and I made adaptations, we had many wonderful and unique meals. My children sometimes said, "This is really good Mom, too bad, we'll never have it again." Whatever was in the refrigerator...what I had on hand, created something different from the original recipe. God clearly taught me living lessons through those cooking experiences. The new ingredients became special and interesting. I discovered interesting ways to stretch hamburger, because I wasn't waiting for perfect conditions.

Adverse Situations and Creative Solutions!

One year we had a pretty bleak Christmas. We all made special gifts for each other. Most of the gifts were gifts of time. It was simple...the kids made little cards saying, "I will take out the trash without being asked for a week." "I will spend time reading to my brother without complaining." We gave each other the gift of time...it was one of those times in our lives that truly made a wonderful memory. I think you would have had to be there to appreciate the sacrifice and the importance of those gifts but maybe you get the jest of the concept! It was during that time that Bill decided we would not answer the phone during meals...and we would just spend time eating our food and sharing good positive encouraging conversation. I still enjoy meals with my family and we enjoy each other...it is not the food, but the community around the table. I love it when Mike and his family come over after church and they bring the food...KFC never tasted so good.

When families face really hard times, the family usually rallies around one another and come to the aid of those members who are facing the difficult time. Is that not a precious time? People call it bonding, I call it responding to the occasion with whatever needs to happen and standing by that family member in times of stress and discouragement. We need to be careful not to judge one another too harshly.

Ecclesiastes 11:7-10
"Light is sweet; it's wonderful to see the sun! When people live to be very old, let them rejoice in every day of life. But let them also remember that the dark days will be many. Everything still to come is meaningless.

Young man, it's wonderful to be young! Enjoy every minute of it. Do everything you want to do; take it all in. But remember that you must give an account to God for everything you do. So banish grief and pain, but remember that youth, with a whole life before it, still faces the threat of meaninglessness!"

Enjoy the moments...enjoy the days, but remember, we will give an account to God for everything we do during our lifetime. How you play the game is very important...and you do win based upon the final curtain call. We win because of what Christ has done for us on the Cross and we win because we have accepted that gift Jesus gave on the Cross. He paid for our sins...all of them. The justice of God has been forever satisfied. God decides when the days are done...and the waiting is really over...and the plan and the purpose is finally final!

> **Ecclesiastes 12:6-7**
> "Yes, remember your Creator now while you are young, before the silver cord of life snaps and the golden bowl is broken. Don't wait until the water jar is smashed at the spring and the pulley is broken at the well. For then the dust will return to the earth, and the spirit will return to God who gave it."

Don't cry over spilled milk. You have time to redeem the days and to set the tone for survival and recovery. You can move forward on a day to day basis. You can claim the promise God made to the Israelites many years ago in the book of Joel. God made a promise to them...that He would restore what they had lost. He reminded them not to be afraid, be glad and rejoice because the LORD has done great things.

Joel 2:25-27
"The LORD says, 'I will give you back what you lost to the stripping locusts, the cutting locusts, the swarming locusts, and the hopping locusts. It was I who sent this great destroying army against you. Once again you will have all the food you want, and you will praise the LORD your God, who does these miracles for you. Never again will my people be disgraced like this. Then you will know that I am here among my people of Israel and that I alone am the LORD your God. My people will never again be disgraced like this.'"

How has this Modern Day Parable helped us to deal with our Waiting Process? This is your second day to accept the challenge to start writing down your thoughts...maybe even praying and asking God to help you deal with your anxiety. Give Him all of your concerns. He is able and we are His!

My Daily
Journal

DAY
2

DAY 3

I'll be there in plenty of time... I'm flying!

I am sure you have heard the statement, "The best laid plans of men and mice, often go amiss." That may not be the exact quote, but you get the jest of what I am saying and where I am going. I had planned to fly up to Duluth for the wedding of my dear friends Shelley and Gerry. I thought to myself, "No Problem!" I was to be the matron of honor and I would surely be there for the rehearsal but to my great surprise and wonder...a huge late winter storm came in.

I got the last flight out of St. Louis and still felt very fortunate and blessed because I thought I could pick up a flight out of Minneapolis to Duluth. Meanwhile, five hours later and sitting on the runway in Green Bay, Wisconsin...I begin to think...this is not at all what I thought it was going to be like. A short trip suddenly became a nightmare in every sense of the word. I had hurried to the airport only to be sitting in a plane in the wrong city and the wrong state with no food!

Don't be afraid of falling as long as you know you can fly. This little phrase took on new meaning for me. I begin to think, "Will I ever get to Minneapolis, and then what?" No planes were landing or getting out. Meanwhile, sitting on the run way in Green Bay, we finally got cleared to fly into Minneapolis but no flights to Duluth were possible until the next day. I would totally miss the rehearsal, now I could only hope I would be there for the wedding.

Cell phones are a gift to us from the Lord...and so are people. I made some calls, with the end results being...total strangers picking me up and driving in the middle of a snow storm and bad roads up to Hinkley, where friends, Georgia and Derek, would pick me up and drive me on to a destination closer but still not my destination. It was now late at night and I indeed had missed the rehearsal but I would make it in time for the wedding.

While wandering around in the airport and trying to catch a flight out, I was riding on the moving escalator in the Minneapolis airport

21

when...a man walked by and said to me..."Hurry Up And Wait!" I was in shock by his statement. I had been thinking that very thought the entire day. I was working on a retreat by that title...and it just freaked me out. I had gotten my opening illustration.

The important thing to remember is, we may miss the rehearsal, but we for sure do not want to miss the main event.

Luke 12:35-40

"Be dressed for service and well prepared, as though you were waiting for your master to return from the wedding feast. Then you will be ready to open the door and let him in the moment he arrives and knocks. There will be special favor for those who are ready and waiting for his return. I tell you, he himself will seat them, put on an apron, and serve them as they sit and eat! He may come in the middle of the night or just before dawn. But whenever he comes, there will be special favor for his servants who are ready!"

"Know this: A homeowner who knew exactly when a burglar was coming would not permit the house to be broken into. You must be ready all the time, for the Son of Man will come when least expected."

Are you ready? I hope you have not grown tired of "Waiting." We know Jesus is coming again and we want to be ready. We want to make sure our confidence is in the finished work of Christ upon the cross. We want to make certain we are prepared and ready.

In your Journaling Moments today...reflect upon those in your life who may not be ready...pray for them and ask God to help them come to grips with missing the rehearsal but not missing the main event. The wedding was such a blessing...and even though there were some details I missed in the rehearsal...it was a beautiful time.

We need to consider if we actually have given our lives to Christ...and our sins have been forgiven...that our relationship with the Father has been established, because we have come to Him through His Son.

John 14:6-7

"Jesus told him, "I am the way, the truth, and the life. No one can come to the Father except through me. If you had known who I am, then you would have known who my Father is. From now on you know him and have seen him!"

Can you remember a time when you hurried and you sat...and you missed what you thought was God's plan. I know that Jesus is coming soon...and you need to know that "today" is the day of salvation. Now is the time to accept Him as your personal Savior. Would you like to pray this prayer right now?

Lord, I know I am a sinner. I need someone, I need Jesus. I don't totally understand all of the business of repentance, or what Christ did on the cross for me...but I need someone in my life on a full-time basis. Please come into my life...and help me to figure this out. I thank You!

Writing your response here would be good. Maybe you have already received Christ into your heart and life. Write Him a love note...and thank Him for dying for your sins. Amen!

My Daily Journal
DAY
3

DAY 4

We've learned to rush but not to wait...

My mother used to constantly say to me, "Hurry Up, you're going to be late! Hurry Edna, Hurry!" I know now that Mom thought of herself as being a slow person and she didn't want me to be late for anything.

Busy, busy, busy...all dressed up and no place to go! Where in the world are we all going? Time Management is a hot topic these days along with Warnings and Signs of Stress! I frankly don't want to admit that activities are running my life. I am much bigger and smarter and more mature than those concepts...aren't you?

We get caught up in the activities...which are for the most part...very good things...but they are running our lives. Some of the warning signs in the life of a stressed out person include, high blood pressure and pounding in the heart. Other visible symptoms...*are you listening?*...dryness of the mouth and throat, headaches, a stiff neck or pain in the lower back, queasiness in the stomach, vomiting or diarrhea, sweating or frequent urination, emotional tension and fatigue, difficulty sleeping, or nervous laughter. *Still listening?*...easily startled, loss of or an excessive appetite, inability to concentrate, difficulty making decisions, withdrawing from others and changes in sexual identity, increased smoking or use of medicines and/or alcohol.

Those things in that list reveal to me I may be a little stressed! We are being forced to look at some of those things on a daily basis. We are being forced to look at what is on our plates and consider if we are doing too much. Remember, "No!" is a spiritual word. Saying yes to things and projects and people can be the beginning of what I call: The Great Rush! Running out the door and spending more time in the Van, remember when families ate together at the same table at the same time of day. Some of these things are early symptoms of living a stressed filled life. We need to get a grip!

I have been working on some important values for the Healthy Family...which by the way, is almost outdated. I still believe some people are out there and they are practicing some of these good

25

values. I want to continue to encourage you to do good things in your family. It doesn't matter if the secular world sees them as valuable or not. God wants to redeem the family and get us back on the right track. Some of those values include the things in the list below:

1. Do you Communicate and Listen?
2. Are you Affirming and Supporting one another?
3. Do you Respect one another?
4. Are you Working on Developing Trust?
5. Do you still Play together and Laugh together? Are you Building Family Memories?
6. Do the members of the Family Share Responsibilities?
7. Are both Parents Involved in Teaching Right from Wrong?
8. Share your Faith with your Family!
9. Admit to Problems and Deal with them...by getting HELP!
10. Value Service to others by Promoting Activities that will Encourage Healthy Service!

You can rush through a lot of things...but you cannot rush a Healthy Family and Christ-like values!

1 Peter 5:6-11
"So humble yourselves under the mighty power of God, and in his good time he will honor you. Give all your worries and cares to God, for he cares about what happens to you!

Be careful! Watch out for attacks from the Devil, your great enemy. He prowls around like a roaring lion, looking for some victim to devour. Take a firm stand against him, and be strong in your faith. Remember that Christians all over the world are going through the same kind of suffering you are.

In his kindness God called you to his eternal glory by means of Jesus Christ. After you have suffered a little while, he will restore, support, and strengthen you, and he will place you on a firm foundation. All power is his forever and ever. Amen."

When we are *rushing and not waiting*...we are not maturing!

We are not learning what is essential for moving forward for the Lord. We need to develop our **knowledge** in order to learn to proceed with wisdom. Our **attitude**, having the "mind and attitude of Christ," gets pushed aside and we move ahead without the gentleness and heart of Christ...which often pours cold water on the spirit of others...and it is not a good thing. Add to the fact, we do not

26

learn any **Skills.** Running around like a bunch of chickens with our heads cut off is basically misguided energy.

Rushing about doesn't teach us to rely upon the Lord rather than our own understanding. It teaches us to act before we think. I have often said to myself, "If I had only waited a little longer I would not have acted so quickly." It is called, open mouth insert foot! Wisdom is not in the action of fools.

In the book of Proverbs...chapter 8, we are reminded how Wisdom is calling out to those who will take the time to listen.

Proverbs 8:34-36
"Happy are those who listen to me, watching for me daily at my gates, waiting for me outside my home! For whoever finds me finds life and wins approval from the LORD. But those who miss me have injured themselves. All who hate me love death."

I know we are rushing around and doing great things, but it is important that we do not *rush for the sake of rushing!* Are we doing the things we are gifted to do? Have we served our families well before running around to serve and do for others while neglecting the needs at home?

Proverbs 19:20
"Get all the advice and instruction you can, and be wise the rest of your life."

You could start today...by writing some of your thoughts about your stress and how you are dealing with it. You could even write a short prayer to remind you to slow down and relax! You might need to get some help for dealing with the Stress Mess in your life? It is never too late to change...or too early to change.

My Daily
Journal

DAY
4

I'm waiting for the will of God... I think?!

DAY 5

If I just wait long enough the right person will come along and my life will be perfect! Even though I wouldn't know if it was the right person or not!

Waiting for the will of God.

Would you recognize it if it hit you in the face? If you are waiting for the bus, you had better make sure you get on the right bus and you have the fare! We can be on the bus taking a very long ride, but going nowhere. It is important to have an idea of our desired destination.

> **Romans 12:1-2**
> "And so, dear Christian friends, I plead with you to give your bodies to God. Let them be a living and holy sacrifice–the kind he will accept. When you think of what he has done for you, is this too much to ask? Don't copy the behavior and customs of this world, but let God transform you into a new person by changing the way you think. Then you will know what God wants you to do, and you will know how good and pleasing and perfect his will really is."

When we come to grips with the Lordship of Christ in our lives...then we can **Trust God to direct our steps!** When we are not copying the behaviors and customs of our society then God can mold us and change how we think and how we act. He will direct our hearts to the things of God and we will be able to test his good and perfect will. Simple, but this may require...

Waiting time...some time of being conformed to His Image and His will for our lives!

Sometimes the "will of God" seems vague. It is hard to know, for myself. I used to think the will of God was something really special...but the will of God is often living our normal everyday lives, which if the truth be spoken...is very special. Each day is a precious gift!

29

Psalm 139:3
"You chart the path ahead of me and tell me where *to stop and rest*. Every moment you know where I am."

Unknown plans for us are often scary...again, it is a matter of trust. If we know Him, then we can trust He is looking out for us and will guide us through to the things we need to do and say. We are to actively seek His will, and to recognize His will for us may also be in the normal everyday happenings of our lives. It is strange when the everyday things become God's plan for our lives. I don't have to call out to God about how I should be serving Him, because I am. I often must choose what is the most important and according to my gifting and priorities I make a choice for that day and that purpose...how freeing for all of us walking in the light of His grace.

James 1:5
"If you need wisdom–if you want to know what God wants you to do–ask him, and he will gladly tell you. He will not resent your asking."

1 John 5:14-15
"And we can be confident that he will listen to us whenever we ask him for anything in line with his will. And if we know he is listening when we make our requests, we can be sure that he will give us what we ask for."

Remember, Waiting is really action...Waiting for God to act in our lives!

Part of the will of God for our lives is obeying His Word. When I get lost and confusion takes over it is because I am not in the Word...I am not listening and obeying the truths of what I already know to be true. Partial obedience is dangerous and we know it, but we aren't always willing to deny ourselves and take up our cross and follow Him. We make choices based upon our will rather than the will of God. It's true...we put our desires ahead of God's desires for our lives. When we ask God to give us the desires of our hearts many times we want our desires to be approved by God. No! It is not going to happen.

If I obey, then I know God will give me the necessary information to make Godly choices. He will support me and he will guide my steps.

Galatians 5:16-25
"So I advise you to live according to your new life in the Holy Spirit. Then you won't be doing what your sinful nature craves.

The old sinful nature loves to do evil, which is just opposite from what the Holy Spirt wants. And the Spirit gives us desires that are opposite from what the sinful nature desires. These two forces are constantly fighting each other, and your choices are never free from this conflict. But when you are directed by the Holy Spirit, you are no longer subject to the law.

When you follow the desires of your sinful nature, your lives will produce these evil results: sexual immorality, impure thoughts, eagerness for lustful pleasure, idolatry, participation in demonic activities, hostility, quarreling, jealousy, outbursts of anger, selfish ambition, divisions, the feeling that everyone is wrong except those in your own little group, envy, drunkenness, wild parties, and other kinds of sin. Let me tell you again, as I have before, that anyone living that sort of life will not inherit the Kingdom of God.

But when the Holy Spirit controls our lives, he will produce this kind of fruit in us: love, joy, peace, patience, kindness, goodness, faithfulness, gentleness, and self-control. Here there is no conflict with the law.

Those who belong to Christ Jesus have nailed the passions and desires of their sinful nature to the cross and crucified them there. If we are living now by the Holy Spirit, let us follow the Holy Spirit's leading in every part of our lives."

The will of God requires waiting for God to lead you...or just support you as you obey what you already know needs to be done. Follow-up is so important. We often know to do good but we simply don't do it...and then of course, it is sin. *Paraphrase from James 4:17*

James 4:8a
"Draw close to God, and God will draw close to you."

Waiting for the right moment to step out in faith requires the discipline of the Holy Spirit. It is not running too far ahead but it is about waiting for the covering of His leadership in our lives.

How has what I have read challenged my Waiting Process? Are you getting tired of me asking you to journal...this is such a healthy way to remember to remember! But of course, No Pressure!

My Daily Journal

DAY 5

DAY 6

Waiting teaches Patience 101... where do I sign up?

The virtue of patience has not been one of my finer qualities. I have discovered over the course of years...patience is a fruit of the Spirit and cannot be called upon from the depths of our own clever devices...no matter how skilled we are in, *looking good!* Patience after all, is one of the by-products of the presence and work of the Holy Spirit who is alive and well in our hearts.

> **Lamentations 3:25**
> "The Lord is wonderfully good to those who wait for him and seek him."

A few years back I was going through one of the many difficult times in my life. My husband had recently passed away and I was about to make a move from Minnesota to Missouri. I was not just moving myself, but I was also moving my Mom. It was a stressful and crazy time. I felt lost and totally overwhelmed with all of the forced changes in my life. I knew it was the will of God, but there was so much work involved with the actual moving process. I had help, but at the end of the day I still had to deal with many choices and they were not all simple, yes or no answers...some involved putting a lot of my life on hold! Waiting and Patience were growing together in my heart and life.

My verse for that year should have been a strong indication of what was ahead for me...

> **Habakkuk 2:3**
> "But these things I plan won't happen right away. Slowly, steadily, surely, the time approaches when the vision will be fulfilled. If it seems slow, wait patiently, for it will surely take place. It will not be delayed."

I know God was telling the prophet Habakkuk the judgement against those who had wronged Israel would come about in time. I took these verses for my own. *If it seems slow, wait patiently, for it will surely take place.* I used to say, I loved the phrase in the Bible that simply said, "This too, shall pass away."

We cannot run from God's plan and purpose for our lives. He is teaching us something in the midst of the difficult trials. Waiting and expectations do not often seem to be on the same page, much less in the same paragraph. It is also true that Waiting and Patience go hand in hand...such a strange combination! I get tired of waiting when I don't see any results...and then to have some person in the wings tell me...you must be learning about patience. Now honestly, do you want to hear that kind of wisdom coming from your friends and family? I think not!

According to the Bible, patience is a form of perseverance and forbearance that allows us to respond to frustrating circumstances with grace and self-control.

So bottom line...waiting is part of growing in the fruit of the Spirit Patience. God is teaching us the ropes for when the difficult times really come...we will then have the fortitude to hang in there until the purpose and final outcome is revealed. It sounds so Spiritual...and Godly...and Righteous...but how does it really play out in our normal, everyday encounters?

I am still in the class room and I am still growing in this area of my life...and you?

Romans 8:25-26
"But if we look forward to something we don't have yet, we must wait patiently and confidently.

And the Holy Spirit helps us in our distress. For we don't even know what we should pray for, nor how we should pray. But the Holy Spirit prays for us with groanings that cannot be expressed in words."

I learn from these verses that I may not understand the process, or the plan or purpose...even then I can be assured that the Holy Spirit will be praying for me to have the understanding and patience I need. Isn't that exciting!

Waiting upon the Lord with confidence...again, it's all about trust and God's faithfulness to His word and to His people. I can learn while I am waiting...even though I may not know the lesson plan. God is always looking after me and His care goes beyond all that I ask or think.

Romans 8:28
"And we know that God causes everything to work together for the good of those who love God and are called according to his purpose for them."

Finally, we come to the meat of the answer. I'm waiting, He knows I am waiting. My assurance and my confidence in not knowing His plan and purpose becomes a top priority for Him...and I can trust that when I need to know, He will get back to me...**as soon as possible**. In the meantime...He is caring for me and loving me and has my best interest in His heart. What a Mighty God we Serve!

Patient endurance...until the time I need to do whatever I need to do...and patient endurance for while I am doing whatever I need to do.

> **2 Peter 1:3-9**
> "As we know Jesus better, his divine power gives us everything we need for living a godly life. He has called us to receive his own glory and goodness! And by that same mighty power, he has given us all of his rich and wonderful promises. He has promised that you will escape the decadence all around you caused by evil desires and that you will share in his divine nature.
>
> So make every effort to apply the benefits of these promises to your life. Then your faith will produce a life of moral excellence. A life of moral excellence leads to knowing God better. Knowing God leads to self-control. Self-control leads to patient endurance and patient endurance leads to godliness. Godliness, leads to love for other Christians, and finally you will grow to have genuine love for everyone. The more you grow like this, the more you will become productive and useful in your knowledge of our Lord Jesus Christ. But those who fail to develop these virtues are blind or, at least, very shortsighted. They have already forgotten that God has cleansed them from their old life of sin."

The Gift of the Holy Spirit in my life is helping me to live my daily life. Equipping me to live the kind of life I want to live and the kind of life that will bring glory to my Father. Amazing!

Resource Concepts for the Waiting Game! What are you learning from the Lord that is helping you to grow in this area of patience...waiting...and depending upon the Holy Spirit. Now that is a scary thought...and your thoughts are?...

My Daily Journal

DAY

6

DAY 7

He'll be with you as soon as possible, have a seat...

They had an opening...I rushed through traffic...my jaw was killing me...and now I was sitting there feeling every throbbing pounding pain in my jaw as it traveled throughout by whole body. Pain...at times it felt like someone was jabbing me with a hot poker or a cold one? I kept telling myself...I am here, now please, please do something FAST! I hoped my Dentist would come to my aid...NOW!

As Soon As Possible...what in the world does that mean to us?

The pain of waiting is sometimes almost unbearable. Waiting can make us bitter and full of unbelief. If someone tells us, "As Soon As Possible," then we have hope, but in the case of Abraham and Sarah, they had waited and waited...and the promised son had not come through the birth canal of Sarah. She became anxious and devised her own plan by having her slave, Hagar bear a son for Abraham. After Hagar had born Abraham a son it was even more apparent to Sarah that she was the source of the problem! After all, Abraham had fathered a child. You can see why she lost hope and she became full of unbelief and yes, bitter!

Genesis 18:1-15
"The LORD appeared again to Abraham while he was camped near the oak grove belonging to Mamre. One day about noon, as Abraham was sitting at the entrance to his tent, he suddenly noticed three men standing nearby. He got up and ran to meet them, welcoming them by bowing low to the ground. 'My lord,' he said, 'if it pleases you, stop here for a while. Rest in the shade of this tree while my servants get some water to wash your feet. Let me prepare some food to refresh you. Please stay awhile before continuing on your journey.'

'All right,' they said. 'Do as you have said.'

So Abraham ran back to the tent and said to Sarah, 'Quick! Get three measures of your best flour, and bake some bread.' Then

37

Abraham ran out to the herd and chose a fat calf and told a servant to hurry and butcher it. When the food was ready, he took some cheese curds and milk and the roasted meat, and he served it to the men. As they ate, Abraham waited on them there beneath the trees."

All the rushing and scurrying about, only to sit and wait beneath the trees! He'll be with you as soon as possible...and with God all things are possible!

BUT...

"'Where is Sarah, your wife?' they asked him.

'In the tent,' Abraham replied.

Then one of them said, 'About this time next year I will return, and your wife Sarah will have a son.'

Now Sarah was listening to this conversation from the tent nearby. And since Abraham and Sarah were both very old, and Sarah was long past the age of having children, she laughed silently to herself. 'How could a worn-out woman like me have a baby?' she thought. 'And when my master–my husband–is also so old?'

Then the LORD said to Abraham, 'Why did Sarah laugh? Why did she say, "Can an old woman like me have a baby?" Is anything too hard for the LORD? About a year from now, just as I told you, I will return, and Sarah will have a son.' Sarah was afraid, so she denied that she had laughed. But he said, 'That is not true. You did laugh.'"

The impossible becomes possible with the Lord...nothing is too hard for Him! We often put limits on God and as we wait we become full of disbelief...we loose faith and trust. We doubt that it is possible and we wonder, will God remember us and our pain and our trials.

Sometimes the answer is yes...and sometimes the answer is no...but God remembers us and He knows everything about us. Remember, He doesn't keep anything from us that is for our good and for His Glory. The Timing is not for us to determine.

The key to growing in patience and our waiting upon the Lord is to develop an eternal perspective. Often the waiting period is part of the passage...or the process that we must go through in order to learn how to persevere. We will gain the skill for future times, at a time when the waiting will be more difficult and we will recall and

38

remember how God got us through those previous times and we will be able to believe that He will indeed get us through the present times. God did it before and He will do it again. It is not about us...it is about His Faithfulness.

I can tell you that when the dentist could see me and he gave me some medication and promised to help me...I was overjoyed! Until you have had a root canal, you will probably never understand this paragraph. There is joy in the Root Canal...knowing that someone can actually help you and give you relief for the pain.

Sarah and Abraham had been waiting for years for that son...the promised one! God's timing is impeccable. He is never late...it may seem slow...but He is never late!

How has this Modern Day Parable helped me deal with my Waiting Process? The Pain of waiting takes on new meaning if it is YOU that is waiting. I used to work in a dentist office and it didn't bother me too much when people called in wanting to see the Dentist...NOW. But, when it became my turn to experience the pain of needing a root canal...I had a totally new perspective and respect for dealing with the situation.

Are you in the midst of a situation...that will not go away. Are you trying to ride it through? I hope someone is available to you to come along side and help you with the pain and waiting...*As Soon As Possible*.

My Daily
Journal

DAY
7

40

DAY 8

Waiting for the cows to come home...

I spent several summers living in the country visiting with my relatives. Every day at about the same time you could look out across the pasture and you would see the cows heading in for the barn. It was like clock work...they just seemed to know when it was best to come into the barn. My cousins and I would get the feed ready in the stalls for them to eat while the milking process was accomplished. Being the city kid that I was...I didn't get it! Milking time for them was necessary and timing was very important to each cow. It wasn't about the food or wanting to be in the barnyard during the evening...it was about needing to be milked for their own comfort and they also wanted to see their calf. It was truly amazing.

The natural way of animals and the changing of the seasons...the Creator God has set things in motion. He decided upon a plan and a purpose of how things should work and how these decisions were guided by the laws of what we call nature. "What you sow, you will reap," for instance. Cows do their thing because that is what they do. They give milk and the timing of all they do is bound by what they produce...milk cows need to be milked twice a day. The cows will not wait. If you don't milk them you will hear them calling your name.

Job 38: 36
"Who gives intuition and instinct?"

Of course, it is God. The Creator God knows all about us and He knows the way of the seasons and the needs of his creatures...great and small.

We know that we can trust God to be faithful to His word. I am so glad He is a Covenant Keeping God.

Psalm 32:8-11
"The LORD says, 'I will guide you along the best pathway for your life. I will advise you and watch over you.

Do not be like a senseless horse or mule that needs a bit and bridle to keep it under control.'

41

Many sorrows come from the wicked, but unfailing love surrounds those who trust the LORD. So rejoice in the LORD and be glad, all you who obey him! Shout for joy, all you whose hearts are pure!"

Obedience and following the Lord has its rewards. When we go out there and try to lead our own lives and follow our own paths it is the way of destruction. It is foolish. When we seek our own will rather than the will of God...or His path that He has prepared for us...we can end up in a very serious place...one that has no path leading home.

Occasionally, a cow would get out of my Uncle's field, but come time for them to be milked they would do whatever to get back to the barn. Sometimes another farmer would bring them home or we would be sent to bring the cow home...and that was not a pleasant experience...dragging that old cow home to be milked. The whole time she would be bawling loud and clear!

We often do not realize how blessed we are to be surrounded by God's unfailing love. Trusting the one who is caring for us is evidence that we have a clear understanding of who God is...and we trust Him with our very lives. Giving ourselves freely to the will and plan of God is not a bad thing.

Psalm 33:18-22
"But the LORD watches over those who fear him, those who rely on his unfailing love. He rescues them from death and keeps them alive in times of famine.

We depend on the LORD alone to save us. Only he can help us, protecting us like a shield. In him our hearts rejoice, for we are trusting in his holy name. Let your unfailing love surround us, LORD, for our hope is in you alone."

David, the shepherd boy who became a King learned to trust God for his life daily. He learned to trust Him as he cared for the sheep. He knew the safety of being in the fold...and the protection of his shield and his staff.

Peter reminds us of this thought:

1 Peter 2:25
"Once you were wandering like lost sheep. But now you have turned to your Shepherd, the Guardian of your souls."

Peter had chosen a different path...he had denied even knowing the

Lord...and still as he was brought back into the fold, he learned that God's love would never leave or forsake him. Sin separates us from the Lord at times. Confession of sin clears away the junk that clutters up our thinking. Getting right with God helps us to think clearly again. We start to remember the truth that Satan is out to get us. He first deceives us and we choose to disobey...when we get our thinking straight...we can then live in spiritual and emotional healing.

> **1 Peter 4:19**
> "So if you are suffering according to God's will, keep on doing what is right, and trust yourself to the God who made you, for he will never fail you."

Waiting for the cows to come home took on a total new meaning for me as I spent time on the farm. Knowing that when I stray and do not follow the path God has for me...the fallout of sin will take its toll. It's the law of nature and of God, what you sow, you will reap...cows want to find the barn in time for milking...it is a primary calling in their lives. We need to walk in the Spirit and obey God's calling in our lives...Obedience is freeing.

I used to think I could get by with something when I was living at home...but somehow my Mom would always find out. I came to believe that parents did indeed have eyes in the back of their heads. When I became a parent, I realized that children want to be found out...they do not enjoy living a double life. They do not really enjoy deceiving and being deceived. They are wanting a day of reckoning. They want to be discovered. We do seek repentance, because we want restoration and healing. A child may enjoy sin for a season, but in due time...the conviction of the Holy Spirit is a strong deterrent and brings us back to the path.

Maybe you have been waiting for some cows to come home. Remember to pray for those friends or family. Trust God to bring them back to the fold. Call them by name and remind them, the pasture is not greener in the other field. Coming home takes courage...sometimes we have to come along side of a wayward cow or lamb, and gently restore that one who has been caught up in sin or been out there in another field.

How has this Modern Day Parable helped us deal with our Waiting Process? How can we come along side of someone else and help restore them back into the joy of their Salvation? Maybe you are the one in need of confession, restoration and healing. God is waiting patiently.

43

My Daily Journal

DAY

8

44

DAY 9

God waited patiently...

This little phrase blows my mind...when I think *God is waiting patiently.*

1 Peter 3:18-21
"Christ also suffered when he died for our sins once for all time. He never sinned, but he died for sinners that he might bring us safely home to God. He suffered physical death, but he was raised to life in the Spirit.

So he went and preached to the spirits in prison–those who disobeyed God long ago when **God waited patiently** while Noah was building his boat. Only eight people were saved from drowning in that terrible flood. And this is a picture of baptism, which now saves you by the power of Jesus Christ's resurrection. Baptism is not a removal of dirt from your body; it is an appeal to God from a clean conscience."

I ask myself, why would God wait for anyone or anything? As I studied this passage I began to think about the task Noah was asked to do...build a boat. God had decided to destroy the whole earth and all those who lived there by a flood...this was not just an ordinary thing that was coming down from the hand of God. It was a new thing, and destroying the earth by a flood was a totally new concept to His children. Noah was the only man who found favor with God...can you imagine it?!

Very similar to the times we are presently living in today!

The earth had become corrupt in God's sight and was filled with violence and sin. People had made poor choices...they continued not to choose God.

Noah had three sons and his sons and their wives came into the safety of the ark. God commanded Noah to bring into the boat two of each kind of every living creature upon the face of the earth. God caused them all to come into the ark. Some additional animals also were invited in...for the purpose of making sacrifices while being housed in this ark. God's provision for life!

45

It had taken a long time to build the ark...and during the time of building, Noah tried to persuade others to join him...but no one did. Eventually the time came to go inside the ark. Noah, his family and the animals went inside the ark...and then, God closed the door. Noah was 600 years old at this time. It had never rained upon the earth before...and then slowly and softly the rain began to fall, it rained and rained for forty days and nights.

I believe God waited for Noah to build the ark granting him time to invite others to join them. He told others of the forthcoming doom. It was a time when people could have repented. They could have chosen to join them in the ark...but no one came. God knew this all the time. He allowed Noah to have this time. God shut the door after everyone was safe inside. The people stood outside and watched, or maybe they didn't watch...maybe they no longer paid any attention to what the crazy old man was doing. They totally ignored the call of God in their lives to repent and turn from sin. It was a critical time in the life of Noah and his family...a time in which God allowed Noah to know he had done all he could do in trying to persuade others to join them.

And Noah would know God had been merciful and waited...he had given them enough time to accept the provision of God but they refused. When people were screaming and calling out, and Noah heard their voices, he would know in his own heart he had done all he could do. Noah would be conscious of the fact that God had given them time to change...but after the door had been shut...it was a done deal.

God waited patiently...

Have you experienced those times in your life when God waited for you to get right with Him...when you watched while God convicted others and brought suffering and pain into their lives, in order for them to have the time to repent...and get back in fellowship with Him. I have watched this process in the lives of others and in my own life as well. God dealing with us in the midst of our poor choices and our total disregard for his Word is a terrible time. I always feel guilty because I couldn't learn about the mercy and grace of God any other way. How foolish I have been.

I am so thankful for God's tenderness...to wait. Noah's conscience was clear...and he felt good about God as well. He remembered God's character could always be trusted. It helped him to feel at peace in his own heart...knowing that everything had been done decently and in order.

46

God knows who will accept His provision and those who will not. I don't know...so I personally try and witness to everyone...telling them and trying to make sure they hear and know the truth of God's Word...what they do with the information is not my responsibility.

Some prepare the soil, some plant, some water, but it is God who will give the increase!

The account of Noah should take us beyond the image of Noah leading the little animals into the Ark, two by two. This is a strong teaching on the total sinfulness of man...and without Jesus having no hope at all. Jesus is the Provision for people today in need of a Savior. The vivid picture in my mind is all those people treading water, hanging on to the trees, climbing to the highest place they could find...but finding no refuge.

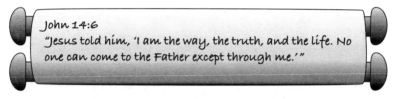

John 14:6
"Jesus told him, 'I am the way, the truth, and the life. No one can come to the Father except through me.'"

We need to pray today for those who we know are outside of the safety of the ark...not willing to repent and come inside the ark. God is calling all who will come to come. Make a list of those you are personally praying for and ask God to give them time to come to Him. Ask for mercy on their behalf...and be faithful to present the truth every time you have an open door! The door has not been closed!

My Daily Journal

DAY
9

Waiting for the promise of the Holy Spirit

What were they waiting for? The Promise of the Holy Spirit...

Acts 1:4-5
"In one of these meetings as he was eating a meal with them, he told them, 'Do not leave Jerusalem until the Father sends you what he promised. Remember, I have told you about this before. John baptized with water, but in just a few days you will be baptized with the Holy Spirit.'"

I sometimes read over my notes before a conference and they seem so dead and flat. No power in those words...flat, dull boring words. I think to myself, this is going to be so boring. "Lord," I pray, "please anoint these words and may your Holy Spirit be the teacher. I am hopeless and helpless without your Spirit's power."

The time for the conference comes...and I get up to speak...and at some point the presence of the Holy Spirit comes and the words take on His power. I get lost in the teaching and caught up in the anointing. I often do not know what I said, or how I said it. Words come, illustrations flow...and God meets us...It is amazing!

Can you imagine trying to go out and fulfill the command, "to go and make disciples," without the filling and the empowering of the Holy Spirit in your life? I cannot imagine it. I am in the process of learning how we may try to do all sorts of things in the *name of Jesus*...but without the Holy Spirit blessing it and using it...we are useless and helpless. I am so afraid to try anything without His empowering, I have learned to face the truth, without the filling of the Holy Spirit, I might as well stay at home. I am worthless without Him.

So often, we say yes to whatever it is we have been asked to do...without any consideration to the idea of thinking about if this is something God has called us to do. We start off without any prayer, we don't seek wise counsel and we wonder why it falls so flat? Is it any wonder? We have way too many programs and plans that are not in the purpose and plan of God for our lives. We build up in our own mind what we think we should be doing without waiting for the Holy Spirit to fill us...to lead and direct us, to teach us what we need to know.

He calms my fears...so I can serve with confidence!

John 14:15-21
"If you love me, obey my commandments. And I will ask the Father, and he will give you another Counselor, who will never leave you. He is the Holy Spirit, who leads into all truth. The world at large cannot receive him, because it isn't looking for him and doesn't recognize him. But you do, because he lives with you now and later will be in you. No, I will not abandon you as orphans–I will come to you. In just a little while the world will not see me again, but you will. For I will live again, and you will too. When I am raised to life again, you will know that I am in my Father, and you are in me, and I am in you. Those who obey my commandments are the ones who love me. And because they love me, my Father will love them, and I will love them. And I will reveal myself to each one of them."

Vs. 23-29 "Jesus replied, 'All those who love me will do what I say. My Father will love them, and we will come to them and live with them. Anyone who doesn't love me will not do what I say. And remember, my words are not my own. This message is from the Father who sent me. I am telling you these things now while I am still with you. But when the Father sends the Counselor as my representative–and by the Counselor I mean the Holy Spirit–he will teach you everything and will remind you of everything I myself have told you.

I am leaving you with a gift–peace of mind and heart. And the peace I give isn't like the peace the world gives. So don't be troubled or afraid. Remember what I told you: I am going away, but I will come back to you again. If you really love me, you will be very happy for me, because now I can go to the Father, who is greater than I am. I have told you these things before they happen so that you will believe them when they do happen.'"

The gift of the Holy Spirit is for our benefit...and He will give us the comfort and strength we need to perform the task of reaching the world with the message of truth and hope.

Paul prayed a prayer for the church and for the Ephesians...

Ephesians 3:16
"I pray that from his glorious, unlimited resources he will give you mighty inner strength through his Holy Spirit."

I know why the disciples waited. Would you want to go out and try and reach the world without the power of the Holy Spirit as your counselor, your guide...and your inner strength? I don't think so!

Ephesians 5:15-20
"So be careful how you live, not as fools but as those who are wise. Make the most of every opportunity for doing good in these evil days. Don't act thoughtlessly, but try to understand what the Lord wants you to do. Don't be drunk with wine, because that will ruin your life. Instead, let the Holy Spirit fill and control you. Then you will sing psalms and hymns and spiritual songs among yourselves, making music to the Lord in your hearts. And you will always give thanks for everything to God the Father in the name of our Lord Jesus Christ."

Let the Holy Spirit fill and control you.

The Spirit-filled life is what we need to seek. We need to be filled with His presence in our lives to be equipped for the ministry and daily living. People controlled by the influence of alcohol gives them a sense of well being...or of power...or they think they have abilities they don't have. When we're controlled by the Spirit, He helps us to face the task with joy, power, courage and strength. We need to be controlled and led by the Spirit of God on a daily basis.

In the matter of Spiritual Warfare, we need the reminder of:

Ephesians 6:10b
"Be strong with the Lord's mighty power."

Maybe you have been out there in the mission field, (your backyard, your neighborhood, your place of business, your school...or, with your family) and you have been approaching the matter without the power of the Holy Spirit's control in your life. Wait and pray and seek His power in your life. We cannot do anything without Him.

Maybe you realized today you have been attempting to do Kingdom work without the power of the Holy Spirit in your life. Confess your sin of trying to do God's work in your own strength and ask for a fresh new filling. Recently we sang in our worship time the old familiar song:

Spirit of the Living God...fall fresh on me. Spirit of the Living God...fall fresh on me. Melt me, mold me...use me, fill me. Spirit of the Living God...fall fresh on me.

Time to pray and ask God to work in your life afresh and anew. It's time to write those thoughts or prayers down.

My Daily Journal

DAY

10

DAY 11

I'm waiting to live for Christ, but not right now...

I met a student once who told me that she was raised a Christian...and she knew she was a Christian, but she wasn't going to be living for the Lord during her College years because she wanted to have some fun. In fact, she said, I am a Christian, but just not practicing my faith at this time.

Luke 11:28
"But even more blessed are all who hear the word of God and put it into practice."

James 2:26
"Just as the body is dead without a spirit, so also faith is dead without good deeds."

I told this young lady...she was in for a terrible four years. She might enjoy a season of fun, but she would experience the loss of joy in her life and she would be robbed of peace. You can only "party" so long before the fiddler must be paid.

It was ironic how she had a roommate who loved the Lord and had all these Bible Studies going on around her...the roommate's Christian friends were always hanging out and laughing, having so much fun at the same time practicing their faith. The Spirit of God finally wore her down and by the end of the semester she was joining her roommate and "their friends" for great times, having fun and studying the Bible. Imagine that!

Waiting to follow the Lord wholeheartedly is a foolish choice...Putting God on hold is dangerous.

Joshua and Caleb, two of my favorite Old Testament characters, followed God with everything they could possibly be about. When the spies went up to spy out the land, they decided not to go in and take over the land because of the giants. The choice...*not to go*, became the decision of the majority...but it was not the wisest choice. That choice carried a curse! The party of disobedience lasted for forty years...a very long time...and lots of funerals!

53

Caleb and Joshua spent 40 years...*Waiting...Waiting and Watching!*

Moses interceded for the people.

Numbers 14:17-30

"Please, LORD, prove that your power is as great as you have claimed it to be. For you said, 'The LORD is slow to anger and rich in unfailing love, forgiving every kind of sin and rebellion. Even so he does not leave sin unpunished, but he punishes the children for the sins of their parents to the third and fourth generations.' Please pardon the sins of this people because of your magnificent, unfailing love, just as you have forgiven them ever since they left Egypt.

Then the LORD said, 'I will pardon them as you have requested. But as surely as I live, and as surely as the earth is filled with the LORD's glory, not one of these people will ever enter that land. They have seen my glorious presence and the miraculous signs I performed both in Egypt and in the wilderness, but again and again they tested me by refusing to listen. They will never even see the land I swore to give their ancestors. None of those who have treated me with contempt will enter it. But my servant Caleb is different from the others. He has remained loyal to me, and I will bring him into the land he explored. His descendants will receive their full share of that land. Now turn around and don't go on toward the land where the Amalekites and Canaanites live. Tomorrow you must set out for the wilderness in the direction of the Red Sea.'

Then the Lord said to Moses and Aaron, 'How long will this wicked nation complain about me? I have heard everything the Israelites have been saying, now tell them this: As surely as I live, I will do to you the very things I heard you say. I, the LORD, have spoken! You will all die here in this wilderness! Because you complained against me, none of you who are twenty years old or older and were counted in the census will enter the land I swore to give you. The only exceptions will be Caleb son of Jephunneh and Joshua, son of Nun.'"

Can you imagine all the funerals Caleb and Joshua had to attend? How many times were they pallbearers and how many times did they wonder...How long Lord, how long?

These men were tested in ways I cannot even imagine. *Hurry Up and Wait...must have been their theme song. It could have been played at every funeral!*

They had come all that distance from the Red Sea and now they headed back in the same direction. They were literally going around in circles. I think forty years must have seemed like a very long time for these two young men who were ready to go in and conquer the promised land, but the majority spoke up. Instead of moving forward...they moved backward and in circles. The ultimate waiting game...and what a feeling of futility?

We have all been there...ready to move forward, ready to do the right thing for God, and then someone stepped in and said, "It can't be done" or "It has never been done this way." It is so hard to wait for others to catch the vision...waiting for them to *get it*. It really does drag us down. How did Caleb and Joshua handle it? Don't you wonder what conversations they had over their tea or coffee...not their Pepsi...that drink is for the generation of the young...and innovative thinkers. It had to be discouraging to them. Waiting for God to bring judgement upon those who were not willing to practice their faith.

How has God spoken to you regarding the need to be about practicing your faith?

My Daily Journal

DAY 11

DAY 12

Are we in the mountains yet?

Our kids really enjoyed being in the car for miles and miles traveling on our vacation trips! NOT!

We were going to the east coast and it was my first trip to see the Atlantic Ocean. I was really excited but the kids were driving me crazy. Their father had told them we had to go through the mountains first, and then we would go to the coast. So, the question, "Are we in the mountains yet?" persisted over the many miles it takes to get from St. Louis to the Atlantic Ocean.

The strange part about this story is when we actually got to the mountains...the climb was so gradual they didn't realize at first we were actually in the mountains. They had been waiting for this special event so they could program their thinking to how close or how far they would be from our final destination.

Waiting for something to happen, an event which you associate to your future or the next event on your social calendar is really hard. We want the details and the time and the events, *to hurry up*. We want to get to the destination. We often forget to enjoy the beauty of the journey because we are so anxious for the final outcome. Can you identify with that concept?

Romans 8:24-27

"Now that we are saved, we eagerly look forward to this freedom. For if you already have something, you don't need to hope for it. But if we look forward to something we don't have yet, we must wait patiently and confidently.

And the Holy Spirit helps us in our distress. For we don't even know what we should pray for, nor how we should pray. But the Holy Spirit prays for us with groanings that cannot be expressed in words. And the Father who knows all hearts knows what the Spirit is saying, for the Spirit pleads for us believers in harmony with God's will."

Our personal freedom in Christ is so evident when we come to know Christ. I have observed those who have been "Worry Warts,"

57

who after they find Christ...actually experience peace and calmness. We have so much in Christ, he really does complete our lives and he renews our minds and our attitudes and our ability to wait. Our salvation is so complete!

Often we want others in our family to come to know Christ in a personal way as well. We pray for them...but we want them to be saved immediately...not thinking about how long it took for the Lord to bring us to the saving knowledge of His grace. We want it yesterday.

A friend of mine was saved and started to pray for his family members. It had been almost six months since his salvation experience and he was chomping at the bit...wanting his family to be saved. I was praying with him...and others too...but he kept wanting it yesterday.

"We must wait patiently and confidently."

We know children can be impatient...but adults are even worse. We have the Holy Spirit praying for us and we have Jesus interceding for us at the right hand of the Father...what a special prayer group! We just become distressed and full of worry. We forget the trip is a major part of the journey.

Confidence in God's wisdom and His ability to keep it all together is a learning process for the new Christian. Over the years, I have become better at waiting, but there are still times when I try to take up the banner and lead the parade. I want to control the outcome and the timing! Yes, I really still get caught up in that trap. I can even want to control others and their decisions. I know this is hard for you to believe because none of you ever experience those kinds of issues in your faith walk, but it does happen. We never seem to outgrow our need to be reminded of the truth we learn in scripture...God knows it all. He has the plan and the purpose and He is in total control of the whole situation.

Look at the next set of verses, which I am sure are very familiar to you.

Romans 8:28-30
"And we know that God causes everything to work together for the good of those who love God and are called according to his purpose for them. For God knew his people in advance, and he chose them to become like his Son, so that his Son would be the firstborn, with many brothers and sisters. And having chosen them, he called them to come to him. And he gave them right standing with himself, and he promised them his glory."

Yes, indeed! "according to his purpose for them."

God has good things planned for us who love Him and are called according to His purpose. I cannot emphasize this point enough, because God makes a point of it over and over again in scripture. It is important to know you are safe and in His will. He will not take you into something that isn't going to be within the limits of His plan. Yes, I know...God has a perfect plan and a permissible plan. I have heard that for years...but if God knows everything, and He does, He also knows the position we will take and the path we will follow. He made the path after all!

God doesn't always make us happy as He is fulfilling His purpose in our lives...but we will be miserable if we stray from that safety net. Our children did not always enjoy the trip...but when they finally got to the ocean, we could hardly get them away from it. They loved the ocean, the rocks and the sand, and the beauty of it all. They still love water and will go to great lengths to enjoy it. My son, Dan, has a pool that is a gathering place for all who enjoy splashing, swimming, and enjoying the cool of the water in hot Mesa, Arizona.

I have rested because of these verses being a major part of my life. I can trust God to be in charge and because I love Him...He is going to direct me. Accepting His will for my life has been a tremendous learning process...acceptance of His will just brings peace in the midst of whatever is going on. "Where He leads me I can follow," has been my main stay in recent years. I can do that...I can go there...I can wait until I have more direction from Him...or more light on the path.

Romans 8:31
"What can we say about such wonderful things as these? If God is for us, who can ever be against us?"

Those words build confidence and assurance in my spirit. They take me beyond my doubts and my fears. The fact that I know God cannot lie just makes them leap right off the page and go straight to my fainting heart. My husband used to say, "the safest place you can be...is in the will of God!"

What more do you require? What more do you want from the Heavenly Father? What He says, He will do! He is a Covenant Keeper, God. He assures me this day...He is taking care of me...always! He cares about my family...those who know Him and those who do not.

Promised Glory...I don't always get that part. I know that is supposed to be the destination. I know that, but I am enjoying some of the Glory and His sweet presence in my life, even today. This morning as I am writing and thinking of this day...I am expecting some of His Glory to be revealed to me TODAY. The journey is happening. I think I may already be in the mountains and I am looking to see how being in His presence today will bring me into the Throne Room of the King!

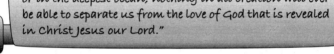

Romans 8:38-39
"And I am convinced that nothing can ever separate us from his love. Death can't, and life can't. The angels can't, and the demons can't. Our fears for today, our worries about tomorrow, and even the powers of hell can't keep God's love away. Whether we are high above the sky or in the deepest ocean, nothing in all creation will ever be able to separate us from the love of God that is revealed in Christ Jesus our Lord."

Do you have family members who need to come to Him? Join with the Holy Spirit and with Jesus and pray for them today.

A symptom of self will and pride is when we do not want to admit we need Him for everything! It is a symptom of spiritual dryness and spiritual neglect.

Journal today about what you might be feeling about God's control verses your control? Why is having God control every aspect of your life so important?

My Daily Journal

DAY

12

Seven years is a long time to wait for the right wife!

DAY 13

Jacob was a rascal...he ran from God and responsibility. He finally met his match! His new father-in-law had something up his sleeve and he proved able to outwit Mr. Jacob.

The story in detail starts in the book of Genesis.

Genesis 25:19-26
"This is the history of the family of Isaac, the son of Abraham. When Isaac was forty years old, he married Rebekah, the daughter of Bethuel the Aramean from Paddan-aram and the sister of Laban. Isaac pleaded with the LORD to give Rebekah a child because she was childless. So the LORD answered Isaac's prayer, and his wife became pregnant with twins. But the two children struggled with each other in her womb. So she went to ask the LORD about it. 'Why is this happening to me?' she asked.

And the LORD told her, 'The sons in your womb will become two rival nations. One nation will be stronger than the other; the descendants of your older son will serve the descendants of your younger son.'

And when the time came, the twins were born. The first was very red at birth. He was covered with so much hair that one would think he was wearing a piece of clothing. So they called him Esau. Then the other twin was born and with his hand grasping Esau's heel. So they called him Jacob. Isaac was sixty years old when the twins were born."

Esau Sells His Birthright to his brother Jacob.

Isaac deceives Abimelech...Isaac being Jacob's father...in Genesis 26

Jacob Steals Esau's Blessing from their father.

Jacob made a vow:

Genesis 28:20-21
"If God will be with me and protect me on this journey and give

me food and clothing, and if he will bring me back safely to my father, then I will make the LORD my God. This memorial pillar will become a place for worshiping God, and I will give God a tenth of everything he gives me."

Jacob arrives in Paddan-aram...meets his future father-in-law.

Jacob agrees to work for his youngest daughter Rachel, for seven years, but when the time came for them to be married...Jacob switched his daughter Leah for Rachel...and so Jacob was married to Leah. He still wanted to marry Rachel...and he worked another seven years for Rachel...(*Hurry up and Wait*) Genesis 29:14-26.

Leah had children and Rachel didn't. Then God allowed Rachel to have a son...and that son's name was Joseph. Isn't it a small world? I am so amazed at the plan and purpose of God.

But the final kick comes in the book of Hosea.

Hosea 12:1-8
"The people of Israel feed on the wind; they chase after the east wind all day long. They multiply lies and violence; they make alliances with Assyria and cut deals with the Egyptians.

Now the LORD is bringing a lawsuit against Judah. He is about to punish Jacob for all his deceitful ways. Before Jacob was born, he struggled with his brother; when he became a man, he even fought with God. Yes, he wrestled with the angel and won. He wept and pleaded for a blessing from him. There at Bethel he met God face to face, and God spoke to him–the LORD God Almighty, the LORD is his name! So now, come back to your God! Act on the principles of love and justice, and always live in confident dependence on your God.

But no, the people are like crafty merchants selling from dishonest scales–they love to cheat. Israel boasts, 'I am rich, and I've gotten it all by myself! No one can say I got it by cheating! My record is spotless.' "

Jacob's name was changed to Israel...and the comings and goings of the nation of Israel has always been an example of our relationship with God. God has to constantly rescue them...over and over again, even as he has to constantly rescue us.

Hosea 13:4
"I am the LORD your God, who rescued you from your slavery in Egypt. You have no God but me, for there is no other savior."

Hosea 14

"Return, O Israel, to the LORD your God, for your sins have brought you down. Bring your petitions, and return to the LORD. Say to him, 'Forgive all our sins and graciously receive us, so that we may offer you the sacrifice of praise. Assyria cannot save us, nor can our strength in battle. Never again will we call the idols we have made "our gods." No, in you alone do the orphans find mercy.'

The LORD says, 'Then I will heal you of your idolatry and faithlessness, and my love will know no bounds, for my anger will be gone forever! I will be to Israel like a refreshing dew from heaven. It will blossom like the lily; it will send roots deep into the soil like the cedars in Lebanon. Its branches will spread out like those of beautiful olive trees, as fragrant as the cedar forests of Lebanon. My people will return again to the safety of their land. They will flourish like grain and blossom like grapevines. They will be as fragrant as the wines of Lebanon.

O Israel, stay away from idols! I am the one who looks after you and cares for you. I am like a tree that is always green, giving my fruit to you all through the year.'

Let those who are wise understand these things. Let those who are discerning listen carefully. The paths of the LORD are true and right, and righteous people live by walking in them. But sinners stumble and fall along the way."

The whole concept of Israel not wanting to follow and obey God is still so true today. We as the body of Christ run at times from God's will. We are very much like the picture of Israel...seeking our own ways...looking unto ourselves for wisdom and counsel. How driven we are by our natural foolish instinct. We have not learned very much when we continue to follow our own thinking and our own ways. God has warned us time and time again...but we do not seem to listen very well at all. We spend so much time doing over and over the same foolish mistakes that others have made before us.

I want to learn from those who have gone before me. I want to profit from their mistakes. I want to have my life count for God. I am in the "second half" of my life and I don't want to continue making the same mistakes.

Can you imagine Jacob...working for 14 years to finally get his bride? I cannot even imagine it! It is the perfect example of hurrying up to achieve something...and then being put on hold until God said, "now it is time." I have rushed, hurried, tried to do it my way...so many times...to only come to the end of myself and say to God, "Please tell me clearly what your will is...so I can obey."

Today as you journal, focus on the times in your life when you have not waited for God and the foolish and wrong distractions that came along and took you down a path that was out there...but the path had no real fruit. Unproductive times when we were spinning our wheels...and going nowhere fast. It is a pitiful time. Repentance is the only thing that clears it all up...and helps us start with a new slate.

Maybe you are in one of those times...and you need to repent NOW...ask for restoration and forgiveness. God is Able...He waits for you to be healed and totally restored. We are His!

My Daily
Journal

DAY
13

DAY 14

Time heals all wounds

I am not really sure I have totally believed in the concept of time healing all of our wounds. Over the years, I have learned that if enough time passes, there will be scars and you can see where the wound was but the scar has replaced the wound. If enough time passes, do we suddenly forget what happened...what was said? I believe the scar is a sign of healing but I am not sure we ourselves are healed of the memories. It may take time for the memories to be released and erased.

With the passing of time...God is able to heal our wounds if we allow him to do so...and we are then free to move forward.

Jacob spent many years working for his father-in-law. Jacob had a dream and the angel of God told him to return to the land he had come from. He packed up his wives, and his live stock and they left. His wives were willing to leave their father because he had reduced their rights to those of foreign women. He had sold them to Jacob and they knew their lot would best be cast with their husband, as their father would never legally give them anything.

Genesis 31:17-21
"So Jacob put his wives and children on camels. He drove the flocks in front of him—all the livestock he had acquired at Paddan-aram—and set out on his journey to the land of Canaan, where his father, Isaac, lived. At the time they left, Laban was some distance away, shearing his sheep. Rachel stole her father's household gods and took them with her. They set out secretly and never told Laban they were leaving. Jacob took all his possessions with him and crossed the Euphrates River, heading for the territory of Gilead."

Laban caught up with Jacob...searched through all of his belongings looking for his household goods but found nothing. Rachel had deceived her father and hid the household items under her saddle on her camel...Laban and Jacob agreed to disagree and Jacob was leaving to return to his homeland.

He had left in a hurry many years ago...due to an argument with his brother Esau about his birthright. Jacob had deceived his father and his brother and now he wanted to return to his people and to his own land...but this guilt was riding along side of him...and as he grew closer to home his conscience started to bother him.

He sent gifts ahead of his arrival to his brother. He was offering a peace offering before his arrival time.

Genesis 32:3-5
"Jacob now sent messengers to his brother, Esau, in Edom, the land of Seir. He told them, 'Give this message to my master Esau: "Humble greetings from your servant Jacob! I have been living with Uncle Laban until recently, and now I own oxen, donkeys, sheep, goats, and many servants, both men and women. I have sent these messengers to inform you of my coming, hoping that you will be friendly to us." ' "

Genesis 33:1-4
"Then, in the distance, Jacob saw Esau coming with his four hundred men. Jacob now arranged his family into a column, with his two concubines and their children at the front, Leah and her children next, and Rachel and Joseph last. Then Jacob went on ahead. As he approached his brother, he bowed low seven times before him. Then Esau ran to meet him and embraced him affectionately and kissed him. Both of them were in tears."

Genesis 33:8-9
"'And what were all the flocks and herds I met as I came?' Esau asked.

Jacob replied, 'They are gifts, my lord, to ensure your goodwill.'

'Brother, I have plenty,' Esau answered. 'Keep what you have.' "

One of the reasons this story is so precious to me is the simple truth of what had happened in the life of Esau. During those 20 odd years that his brother had been gone. He didn't seek revenge...he had moved on in his own life. He had not allowed the past to interfere with the present and his hope of a future...and now he could say, "Brother, I have plenty." Contentment had come into his life.

As long as we seek revenge, we cannot be healed. We must come to a place of contentment and God will supply the peace.

Personally, if I do not seek forgiveness first with the Lord...then with others, "as much as it is possible be at peace with all men." Hebrews

12:14, I can be sure I am not going to be able to move forward. I will stay in that one spot until God deals with me. I am very stubborn and have had to learn to release the pain before God could actually heal my broken spirit.

It is not about whose fault it is...or who is responsible for the transgression, it is about seeking resolution and healing. This process is the key to our living in His Presence!

- **Confession and Repentance**
- **Caring Enough to Confront**
- **Forgive and Release**
- **Healing and Restoration can Begin**
- **Resolution!**

It is not about settling the score or rebuking the person or getting even...or bitterness and resentment...it is about seeking healing. God wants us to have peace and contentment in our lives. The scar reminds us of the pain...but it also reminds us of the healing.

Jacob had cheated his brother Esau and Laban had cheated Jacob...and on it went. It had to stop at some point. There comes a time when revenge is not worth the effort. It has to end.

When I read in the passage, they both cried, both brothers bore the responsibility of the sin. I could see they were both truly healed. Esau had moved on...and Jacob had to come home to make this situation right with his brother. It was a Kodak moment! It was a time of repentance and release...letting go of the past so they could live in the present and have hope for the future.

Many nights as Jacob tended his sheep and watched over his flocks he remembered and he had no real rest or peace until he settled it with his brother face to face. How long is long enough?

Time does heal some wounds...and the broken pieces can often be mended. It may take time. It may take growing up and getting a reality check in our lives. It saddens me when families spend years not getting along...not forgiving one another.

It is not about waiting for the other person to make the first move. It is stepping out and realizing that forgiveness starts with YOU.

You will be the one to choose to live in peace. The other person may not be willing to forgive and release...but you can model it for your

71

children and those in your circle of friends. You may need to walk in obedience and take the first step...and you may not be forgiven or acknowledged but you have done the best you can do. God will honor those steps of faith.

This Moment For Journaling is a serious step. Looking at the scar, realizing the healing has partially taken place...but consider if you need to do anything else to move the process forward to restoration...you will have to do it. Ask God to direct you and lead you in the right steps as you seek contentment and healing.

Pray for others in your family for healing. Those memories that have hurt you over the years can now be released and healed.

Isaiah 53:5
"But he was wounded and crushed for our sins. He was beaten that we might have peace. He was whipped, and we were healed!"

Present tense...we are healed! Praise God. It is under the blood...we are forgiven, restored, and forever healed. Nothing that has ever happened to us is unknown to our Heavenly Father. He provides for our burdens to be erased...blotted out forever. Next Phase...contentment and peace!

My Daily Journal

DAY

14

DAY 15

Waiting in line...

I was standing in line...once again. Sometimes I think the lines in grocery stores have only one purpose...to test our patience. I was glad for the fact, the line was moving ever so slowly. It wasn't that I was having any dire emergency...or had to be someplace...I was after all, shopping for groceries and that takes time and that is just how it is.

I have found myself waiting for God to move many times. It feels like I am waiting in line for God to take my call...or for my turn to be next. Can you identify? Have you noticed when you are waiting for something to happen in your life it seems like everyone and their brother are ahead of you and your turn is into next week! It can seem like there is no answer and God may be on His lunch hour.

Psalm 27:14
"Wait patiently for the LORD. Be brave and courageous. Yes, wait patiently for the LORD."

Yes, of course it has to be repeated...because the first time around...we just don't get it.

Psalm 28:1-2
"O LORD, you are my rock of safety. Please help me; don't refuse to answer me. For if you are silent, I might as well give up and die. Listen to my prayer for mercy as I cry out to you for help, as I lift my hands toward your holy sanctuary."

David must have felt he was in the wrong line. He was calling out to God for help. He was asking God to come to his aid. We have all been there. His self talk was really good at this point when he reminded himself, *to be brave and courageous!*

Little children must get discouraged when they keep asking Mom or Dad for something and the reply is...*In just a minute!*

I have said that little statement to my children when they were young and also to my grandchildren. I carried that little phrase through two generations. It is really a holding statement. Everything continues to go on, but you get a little reprieve...*IN A MINUTE*...and our voice gets a little stronger...but the children know...it is never, *just a minute!*

In of ourselves, we might not follow through with what the children want...but we can be sure God hears us. First of all, He does care about what concerns us. And secondly, if it is His will, He will do it...simply because He delights in giving His children the desires of their heart. When our desires are consistent with the will of God the answer seems to come quickly. When our desires are inconsistent with the will of God the answer comes in the form of, NO...Not Now...Maybe, Just Keep Waiting.

Standing in line...waiting for the Will of God.

Things we need to remember while standing in line...The Lord is our rock and safety. The Lord hears us and He will not be silent. We can trust Him, we can call out for His mercy.

> **Psalm 28:9**
> "Save your people! Bless Israel, your special possession! Lead them like a shepherd, and carry them forever in your arms."

I sometimes say this when I am thinking of this verse: I call it, Edna's paraphrase!

"Save me...Bless me...because I am your special possession. Be my shepherd and carry me in your arms to safety."

Hurry Up And Wait...while I am waiting, Lord! Could you please Hurry Up! Isn't that how we want God to be. We have no patience for His will...and we want His will to come quickly. I often have to remind myself, "God's timing is impeccable."

One of the reasons God tells us to be courageous is because when we are waiting we are afraid of what is ahead. The unknown is difficult...it takes on the feeling of mystery and perhaps darkness. We cannot see what is ahead and we feel insecure, tense and a bit at a loss. We ask the questions, but find no real solutions to our dilemma. We ask, what now?

Psalm 27:1
"The Lord is my light and my salvation–so why should I be afraid? The Lord protects me from danger–so why should I tremble?"

Waiting for the results of my Mom's breast biopsy was one of those times. Thinking about the possibilities and the unknown...the uncharted waters...it was a fearful time. Mom, on the other hand, was calm and gave me words of encouragement. She had been in this place before and reminded me again of a phrase my husband said often, "Nothing can happen to us, outside of the will of God." It helped and reassured me once again to remain peaceful. I was living in the Light and He was aware of everything.

The Journaling today is about your life. What things are you waiting for God to do in your behalf. Waiting for the results of a test. Are you waiting in line...or have you just been served? Maybe you need to thank him for his peace during this time and remind yourself to be courageous because God is in control of all circumstances and situations.

A friend who has been very ill for months, has been waiting...waiting for his disease to go into remission. Waiting for God to take care of his physical needs. The call finally came...the terrible disease is in remission. We laughed and almost cried...remembering, He delights in giving His Children Good Things!

What a relief. Sometimes the waiting doesn't give us the desired results...then what? Will we remember our God is in control...and our days and lives belong to Him.

My Daily
Journal

DAY
15

If you wait for perfect conditions, you will never get anything done.

DAY 16

We quoted this verse early on in the Journaling Moments and now we want to focus on this concept even more.

I have not been known for being a person with a "perfectionist problem." Obviously, I want to do things well, but I know in my heart of hearts it will never be perfect. I can do a lot of things, but none of them have ever been perfect. I can survive with "well done, thou good and faithful servant"...but I am NOT the woman of Excellence. I get a lot done, and hopefully enjoy the journey as I go.

The Pitfalls of Perfectionism cause many a good woman and man to fall.

+ Comparing ourselves with the accomplishments of others.
+ Allowing our insecurities to block our dependence upon the Lord.
+ Thinking that our performance will make us more spiritual or favored by the Lord.
+ Seeing the negative aspects of our accomplishments rather than seeing the good.
+ Thinking that we will be loved more if we are perfect.
+ Believing we can be perfect.

Ecclesiastes 11:5-6
"God's ways are as hard to discern as the pathways of the wind, and as mysterious as a tiny baby being formed in a mother's womb.

Be sure to stay busy and plant a variety of crops, for you never know which will grow–perhaps they all will."

Failure has been a good teacher for my life. When I started cooking or learning to cook...the concept of try and try again became my theme song. I actually have become a very good cook over the years but a lot of practice came into play during those learning years. My family ended up with eating a lot of the failures. Not so good...burnt ones...as the children used to refer to some of the cooking samples I gave out. God built into me the ability to "stay by the stuff." When the project becomes difficult I discovered, I could call for help, find someone who could do it with me or even for me, if they were willing. I could find someone to do it, and then pay them, or I could read the directions!

I love those projects which state clearly how simple the directions are to follow and then you find they are written in several different languages...none of which you can read or speak...it is like finding yourself on a different planet...all alone!

I have tried doing some of those projects on my own and they end up being a disaster. One fun time in my life, and a great memory now, was when Bonnie Bass and I decided we could put simple shelves together. We laughed and laughed and when we finally got them together they just sort of leaned like the, "Leaning Tower of Pisa!" We had bolts and screws left over...it was pitiful...but someone came to our rescue and really got them together. I learned that failure could be a learning experience. NEVER AGAIN SHOULD I ATTEMPT PUTTING SHELVES TOGETHER. I could get someone else to help me...or not have shelves. I used to call Melanie Spencer when it got really bad! HELP!

Perfectionism doesn't allow for us to be able to admit we can't... or even call for help! The body of Christ never gets to assist perfectionists, because they never need any help...they can do it all. I know that isn't true...and deep down inside of you, you know it is as well. One of the great truths about being in the body of Christ is this:

I need you...and you need me. We can do it Together!

1 Corinthians 12:12-27
"The human body has many parts, but the many parts make up only one body. So it is with the body of Christ. Some of us are Jews, some are Gentiles, some are slaves, and some are free. But we have all been baptized into Christ's body by one Spirit, and we have all received the same Spirit.

Yes, the body has many different parts, not just one part. If the foot says, 'I am not a part of the body because I am not a hand,' that does not make it any less a part of the body. And if the ear says, 'I am not part of the body because I am only an ear and not an eye,' would that make it any less a part of the body? Suppose the whole body were an eye–then how would you hear? Or if your whole body were just one big ear, how could you smell anything?

But God made our bodies with many parts, and he has put each part just where he wants it. What a strange thing a body would be if it had only one part! Yes, there are many parts, but only one body. The eye can never say to the hand, 'I don't need you.' The head can't say to the feet, 'I don't need you.'

In fact, some of the parts that seem weakest and least important are really the most necessary. And the parts we regard as less honorable are those we clothe with the greatest care. So we carefully protect from the eyes of others those parts that should not be seen, while other parts do not require this special care. So God has put the body together in such a way that extra honor and care are given to those parts that have less dignity. This makes for harmony among the members, so that all the members care for each other equally. If one part suffers, all the parts suffer with it, and if one part is honored, all the parts are glad.

Now all of you together are Christ's body, and each one of you is a separate and necessary part of it."

Maybe one of the reasons we can't do things perfectly is because we would never require the aid and help of others in the body of Christ. What a blessing it is to have the body working together and all depending upon the Lord and each other.

One is a lonely number...and we do need each other. I need you, and you need me. I cannot do it myself. If I could, I would try. What a disaster that would be! I know there are things in my life that I must take responsibility for as I grow in my faith walk with the Lord. I do have to do some things on my own...but I have to also depend upon the Lord for everything. I can do anything in the strength God provides...that is a basic Biblical truth we all need to practice in our Christian lives. I am nothing without Him...but with the Lord...I am able to accomplish His plan and purpose for my life.

> ### Romans 12:4-6
> "Just as our bodies have many parts and each part has a special function, so it is with Christ's body. We are all parts of his one body, and each of us has different work to do. And since we are all one body in Christ, we belong to each other, and each of us needs all the others.
>
> God has given each of us the ability to do certain things well."

What is your part? What is mine? I can give to you my gift...and you can give to me your gift and together we glorify God our Father.

Journaling Moment Today is focused on not being perfect...but being a healthy part of His Body and how you can bring Glory and Honor to the Father and serve others with your gifts.

My Daily
Journal

DAY
16

DAY 17

The rabbit and the turtle

We all remember that funny little story we used to read to our children about the little rabbit that was in a race with the turtle...actually, I think it was called the Hare and the Tortoise.

The rabbit races ahead and gets so bored because the turtle is so far behind...he takes a snooze, he goes off into the fields and just flits about here and yon...while the little turtle plots his course and stays on task...finally finishing ahead of the silly rabbit.

What is the theme we are supposed to be learning from this little fable...who knows? I think parents often read these stories and make up the example to be anything they want it to be. I might be guilty of doing that myself...but please do not tell my children!

There is a lot to be said, for staying on course...but there is a lot to be said, about being able to take time out and rest or just do something for fun. Depending on the fact if you are at work and need to give your employer a full days work...or if indeed, you are just doing a silly race. We all need days off...and time off...and once in awhile we need to go off into the woods and explore the world.

We all need to focus on what the purpose of our journey might be and then do it, but we can also take time out. Couples get so involved with living, making money, their careers, raising the kids...they often neglect the relationship they share as husband and wife. Life is not about a race...racing through this stage and on to the next stage as we go. It is also about enjoying the moments...embracing the race.

We applaud the turtle for continuing on and being faithful to complete the task...and the bragging foolish rabbit. He didn't finish the race in first place. Both needed to learn a lesson. The turtle learned he could do it...and the rabbit bragged before he had actually won the race.

Accepting where we are and who we are is a major growth concept. I can do many things. I am gifted to do some things well...but there are times when God calls me to do something and I feel ill equipped and not really suited for the task...and then God reminds me of the story in the Old Testament, a favorite of mine for following up and completing the task.

Nehemiah reminded those who were opposing the building of the walls to remember something about God.

Nehemiah 4:14
"Then as I looked over the situation, I called together the leaders and the people and said to them, 'Don't be afraid of the enemy! Remember the Lord, who is great and glorious, and fight for your friends, your families, and your homes!' "

Sometimes we are taken beyond our fear and we remember who God is...and what we are fighting for and we receive courage and energy. Today, we cannot give up or give in...we are fighting for our friends, and our families and our homes. We must stay on course. We have to finish the race because others are counting on us. The Victory is ours because of the Lord!

2 Corinthians 1:8-11
"I think you ought to know, dear friends, about the trouble we went through in the province of Asia. We were crushed and completely overwhelmed, and we thought we would never live through it. In fact, we expected to die. But as a result, we learned not to rely on ourselves, but on God who can raise the dead. And he <u>did deliver us</u> from mortal danger. And we are confident that <u>he will continue to deliver us.</u> He will rescue us because you are helping by praying for us. As a result, many will give thanks to God because so many people's prayers for our safety have been answered."

1 Corinthians 1:26-29
"Remember, dear brothers and sisters, that few of you were wise in the world's eyes, or powerful, or wealthy when God called you. Instead, God deliberately chose things the world considers foolish in order to shame those who think they are wise. And he chose those who are powerless to shame those who are powerful. God chose things despised by the world, things counted as nothing at all, and used them to bring to nothing what the world considers important, so that no one can ever boast in the presence of God."

The Lord chooses us based upon His strength...in our weakness, His strength is made perfect. I don't think I can walk a block...I know
84

this to be true...but with God's help, I can finish the race. He takes me from the beginning until I reach the finish line.

The rabbit brags about how his life is so together...and he predicts his successes one after another. He runs with confidence and is basically a "show off," but the day of reckoning will come along and he will have to deal with a point in time...when someone will outdo him, out smart him, and all he is left with is the results...what really went down. Aren't you thankful for the grace of God in your life? When you blow it...you can be forgiven. There are times, when we do have to live with the results of our poor choices and others around us must live with those results as well. We need to be careful not to brag too loud and to honestly deal with the matter of pride.

I pray for the mind of Christ in discerning if I am a rabbit or a turtle.

1 Corinthians 2:11-16

"No one can know what anyone else is really thinking except that person alone, and no one can know God's thoughts except God's own Spirit. And God has actually given us his Spirit (not the world's spirit) so we can know the wonderful things God has freely given us. When we tell you this, we do not use words of human wisdom. We speak words given to us by the Spirit, using the Spirit's words to explain spiritual truths. But people who aren't Christians can't understand these truths from God's Spirit. It all sounds foolish to them because only those who have the Spirit can understand what the Spirit means. We who have the Spirit can understand these things, but others can't understand us at all. How could they? For, 'Who can know what the Lord is thinking? Who can give him counsel?' But we can understand these things, for we have the mind of Christ."

It is a serious matter to determine what the race is...where you are going and why are you racing and running. Be sure you have your priorities in order.

Journal today for a few moments about your life...where you are going? What you are actually doing and if indeed you are doing what God has called you to do? How will you apply these truths to your heart and your family? God wants us always to make the application to the practical aspect of who we are IN CHRIST.

My Daily
Journal

DAY
17

DAY 18

Time share...

Time Share is a very big part of our world today. It is amazing all of the people who own and share vacation homes. They share the ownership and the expenses and the time when they can come and enjoy the beauty of living on the beach for several weeks at a time or even longer periods of time within that year based upon the contract. But if you want to share the time at the same time...there is a conflict.

This is also true in our relationship with God. We cannot just give God part of our time. God wants all of us. God wants us to be His servants all of the time...Twenty-four Seven as they say. But the conflict comes when we want to do it our way...and we start to live our lives as though it is our time and God is on a Time Share Plan. This concept simply will not work.

The Lord clearly speaks to us about our money...or treasures...and the time it takes to build up those treasures. He talks about not being able to add a moment to our lives. These are matters of how we manage our time and what our priorities are concerning our service to and for Him.

Matthew 6:24
"No one can serve two masters. For you will hate one and love the other, or be devoted to one and despise the other. You cannot serve both God and money."

Matthew 6:27
"Can all your worries add a single moment to your life? Of course not!"

Matthew 6:30
"And if God cares so wonderfully for flowers that are here today and gone tomorrow, won't he more surely care for you? You have so little faith!"

Matthew 6:34
"So don't worry about tomorrow, for tomorrow will bring its own worries. Today's trouble is enough for today."

Worry is a distraction from serving God on a full-time basis. When we start looking around us at what we have or do not have we start to spend more time on coveting those things rather than putting God first in our lives and trusting Him to supply our needs. We are *time sharing with our daily concerns rather than trusting God for our daily needs.*

The cost of following Jesus is huge. He wants our undivided attention. He wants our focus to be on serving Him and not the cares of this life. He paid in full...for the whole bag of enchiladas. We are not bargaining with God again for His rights and our rights. People get so caught up in giving God what he already owns. He is the property owner. He has all of the rights.

Matthew 8:18-22
"When Jesus noticed how large the crowd was growing, he instructed his disciples to cross to the other side of the lake.

Then one of the teachers of religious law said to him, 'Teacher, I will follow you no matter where you go!'

But Jesus said, 'Foxes have dens to live in, and birds have nests, but I, the Son of Man, have no home of my own, not even a place to lay my head.'

Another of his disciples said, 'Lord, first let me return home and bury my father.'

But Jesus told him, 'Follow me now! Let those who are spiritually dead care for their own dead.'"

Those are powerful words, forsaking all others to follow Him. Giving Him our total amount of time...all of our lives.

Romans 12:1-3
"And so, dear Christian friends, I plead with you to give your bodies to God. Let them be a living and holy sacrifice–the kind he will accept. When you think of what he has done for you, is this too much to ask? Don't copy the behavior and customs of this world, but let God transform you into a new person by changing the way you think. Then you will know what God wants you to do, and you will know how good and pleasing and perfect his will really is."

Romans 13:11-14
"Another reason for right living is that you know how late it is; time is running out. Wake up, for the coming of our salvation

is nearer now than when we first believed. The night is almost gone; the day of salvation will soon be here. So don't live in darkness. Get rid of your evil deeds. Shed them like dirty clothes. Clothe yourselves with the armor of right living, as those who live in the light. We should be decent and true in everything we do, so that everyone can approve of our behavior. Don't participate in wild parties and getting drunk, or in adultery and immoral living or in fighting and jealousy. But let the Lord Jesus Christ take control of you, and don't think of ways to indulge your evil desires!"

Time is Running Out!

Right living, and living in the light. We need to realize the truth, the night is upon us and we need to be aware that our time is running out...what we do for Christ is after all, what really counts. How are you doing? Are you sharing your life with Christ...or are you giving him total control of your life? Important questions that cause us to think deeply about where we are with this matter of, *Lordship of Christ!*

People often tell me...I am a Christian, but I am so busy I can't possibly serve God, do my job and raise my family. I want to be where you are and eventually, I will be where you are...but for NOW...I want to enjoy my life and do what I have to do. Life is short and I have all these things going on.

They don't actually say it...but what they are saying is:

"I am doing a time share with the Lord right now, and this is my time."

How sad. You cannot convince anyone that what is happening in their lives is self-destructive. You cannot say, STOP...get a grip. You don't really want to do this...or can you? Self talk is good. Maybe you should be self talking to yourself today about sharing your life with Christ rather than giving your life totally to Him.

A marriage will not succeed unless each partner gives themselves totally to the Lord first, and then to each other. It will not work...being a part-time marriage partner and a part-time Mom...and a part-time Christian. We have to make some choices!

Romans 14:17-19
"For the Kingdom of God is not a matter of what we eat or drink, but of living a life of goodness and peace and joy in the Holy Spirit. If you serve Christ with this attitude, you will please God.

And other people will approve of you, too. So then, let us aim for harmony in the church and try to build each other up."

Romans 14:23c
"If you do anything you believe is not right, you are sinning."

James 4:17
"Remember, it is a sin to know what you ought to do and then not do it!"

Journal today about your life and where you are with the Lord in this matter of Time Share. Maybe you are totally sold out to Him...what a good thing. Journal then about how your life is complete and full and you are feeling surrounded by His peace and joy. *It's Your Turn To Share!*

My Daily Journal

DAY
18

DAY 19

Time...to spare

One thing about having time to spare, it gives you a chance to relax and watch people...or you can take a nap...or you can just sit and "veg!" Which I think is an art. Often, we fill up the blanks in our Day Timers with something we feel is productive. We make some phone calls, we start working on tomorrow's meetings or tomorrow's concerns. What do you do with, "Time to Spare?"

Getting to a destination before the game starts...having margins in our lives is a bonus. We have time to relax and wait for the next event. I carried all of my children ten months. I had more time to prepare and be ready for their arrival...but did I enjoy that extra time...NO! I was anxious, my husband would take me on long walks thinking that would encourage the birth of our sons. What it did do for me...was make me exhausted and even more anxious. I was trying to do it on time...but didn't have a clue. One week I had been to the hospital three times with false labor. When I finally went into labor, Bill stopped in the park on the way to the hospital asking me once again, was I sure I needed to go...and would I promise to have the baby this time! Like I had anything to do with anything!

We are a generation that basically doesn't know what to do with Time to Spare. We become concerned with what to do with the extra time. It becomes a concern rather than a time to enjoy the moments. We are crazy! We are driven to make the most of every waking moment.

We hurry up and wait...but have no understanding of how to relax!

Extra time, causes us more tension. I am guilty of high stress while waiting in airports! Waiting has become a challenge. What do we do during those extra hours? Being creative is important. We must use every moment and make every moment count. Where does that philosophy come from? Who designed this kind of thinking, *we have to be busy all the time?* Certainly God didn't model that for us...He did His creative thing...and then He rested. I love it!

Use your bible to read about it in **Genesis 1-2:3**. Also read **Leviticus 25:1-7**. Even the land is to have a year of total rest.

The scripture talks about the year of Jubilee...and allowing debtors to be set free from the burden of their debts. The land is to be free to replenish the nutrients for the soil. Time to spare may be a good thing for a person whose life is ruled by appointments and deadlines. We often need a break from the daily routine...a little time out! It can produce refreshment and diversion. We need both.

We anticipate the next day and the next hour...and even the next moment. We don't know how to simply take life in stride and enjoy the view. We get caught up in our concerns, programs, and our time frame. I think we should keep appointments. I am the first to tell you, I have a planner. I couldn't exist without a schedule. There is freedom in structure...but I am also learning not to plan my world so much, I miss out on some spontaneous time. I don't know what tomorrow will bring into my life...much less, the next moment...but I am learning to enjoy the view from where I am sitting. I want to take pleasure in the journey as I am moving toward the destination.

Proverbs 27:1
"Don't brag about tomorrow, since you don't know what the day will bring."

II Peter 3:8-9
"But you must not forget, dear friends, that a day is like a thousand years to the Lord, and a thousand years is like a day. The Lord isn't really being slow about his promise to return, as some people think. No, he is being patient for your sake. He does not want anyone to perish, so he is giving more time for everyone to repent."

God gives us time to spare for a reason. He has a plan and a purpose for our lives and each day is a gift...each moment of time is a precious gift of time...I need to remember to enjoy the moment.

I know we are to redeem the time and to take advantage of our gifts of time. I also know we can rest and enjoy our time as well. Balance in life is always important. The days are evil...and people do need to hear about Jesus...but sometimes, I can take some time out to just enjoy what is happening around me.

I need to seek to make my life what Christ wants it to be. I know that...but I am not going to feel all guilty about having some extra time in my life. If I daily ask the Lord for His guidance, I know that the whole day belongs to Him.

When was the last time you had a few minutes to just enjoy the beauty of the day...or watch your children play? When was the last time you took a nap and felt refreshed...because you had a few moments to spare?

Journal today, if you have a moment, about God's gifts of time to you and thank Him for this special Journaling moment...to just be!

My Daily Journal

DAY

19

DAY 20

Waiting...is an art form

Some people are just so together! They can make simple things seem elegant. You know someone that fits this description...it may even be you! I watch people as they wait. They are not just waiting, they are making the most of the time and doing it with some style or purpose.

I think the reason some people make such good use of their time is because they are balanced and have taken the time to make moments for relaxation and rest as well as being productive and creative.

I watch people in the airports as I wait for the next flight. Some of them, I call *performers*. We are all waiting after all...but they bring a snack...or piece of pizza, they have napkins, drinks and sometimes those cloth wipe things for their children. One lady was knitting, another was sewing or stitching, another person was doing their nails, and another cleaning out her purse. That one caught my eye for sometime...all the stuff she piled in a neat little pile and then threw it in the trash can! Some wait in the little pubs and watch the latest news on the television as they consume their favorite beverage. Some play cards and just visit. Lovers who sit and hold hands and quietly look deep into the eyes of the other. I have no idea what they might be discussing...probably really important things...like their grades...or what classes they will be taking next semester. These people were not waiting all in the same two hours...but over the course of a year, you start to think you could see it all. We are all performers waiting to be called upon to play our parts.

There was one who really intrigued me. It was a gal with her little dog. It was one of those little dogs with lots of hair. I don't know the breed but it was in a little cage...she had a blanket and a pillow for the little dog. His toys were in there and a water cup and food cup. The little dog was ever so calm looking out of the wired cage watching everything and everyone. He was interested in everything happening around him or her.

The woman asked when the plane was scheduled to load and the lady behind the counter informed her in about twenty minutes. She gave the little dog his tranquilizer and it was a done deal. He sat there for several minutes and then just slowly laid down and was out...now that is waiting with no purpose or plan. The woman told me, he would wake up around their arrival time and would not be stressed or anxious. She traveled with her little pet all the time...and the tranquilizer did the trick.

The ability to wait and continue to accomplish a purpose is an art form. Some people are on their cell phones, others are working on projects on their lap tops, some talk to their brokers or families, some sleep on the floor...in the chairs...they drape their legs over the arms of the seats and look almost comfortable. They have pillows or use clothing to prop up their heads...it's an art!

Waiting for the Lord's Second Coming is an Art Form.

I Thessalonians 4:13-18
"And now, brothers and sisters, I want you to know what will happen to the Christians who have died so you will not be full of sorrow like people who have no hope. For since we believe that Jesus died and was raised to life again, we also believe that when Jesus comes, God will bring back with Jesus all the Christians who have died.

I can tell you this directly from the Lord: We who are still living when the Lord returns will not rise to meet him ahead of those who are in their graves. For the Lord himself will come down from heaven with a commanding shout, with the call of the archangel, and with the trumpet call of God. First, all the Christians who have died will rise from their graves. Then, together with them, we who are still alive and remain on the earth will be caught up in the clouds to meet the Lord in the air and remain with him forever. So comfort and encourage each other with these words."

I Thessalonians 5:1-11
"I really don't need to write to you about how and when all this will happen, for you know quite well that the day of the Lord will come unexpectedly, like a thief in the night. When people are saying, 'All is well; everything is peaceful and secure,' then disaster will fall upon them as suddenly as a woman's birth pains begin when her child is about to be born. And there will be no escape.

But you aren't in the dark about these things, dear brothers and sisters, and you won't be surprised when the day of the Lord comes like a thief. For you are all children of the light and of the day; we don't belong to darkness and night. So be on your guard, not asleep like the others. Stay alert and be sober. Night is the time for sleep and the time when people get drunk. But let us who live in the light think clearly, protected by the body armor of faith and love, and wearing as our helmet the confidence of our salvation. For God decided to save us through our Lord Jesus Christ, not to pour out his anger on us. He died for us so that we can live with him forever, whether we are dead or alive at the time of his return. So encourage each other and build each other up, just as you are already doing."

As you and I wait for the Lord to return, I wonder how we are doing? Have we become complacent? Are we busy living our lives without any interest or concern about the things of God and what is going on around us...in our neighborhoods, our places of business and our schools? Do we consider those around us who may be lost and need to know about Jesus and His second coming? They don't even understand the first coming...we have to catch them up on so much...are you sleeping this time away?

II Thessalonians 2:1-15
"And now, brothers and sisters, let us tell you about the coming again of our Lord Jesus Christ and how we will be gathered together to meet him. Please don't be so easily shaken and troubled by those who say that the day of the Lord has already begun. Even if they claim to have had a vision, a revelation, or a letter supposedly from us, don't believe them. Don't be fooled by what they say.

For that day will not come until there is a great rebellion against God and the man of lawlessness is revealed–the one who brings destruction. He will exalt himself and defy every god there is and tear down every object of adoration and worship. He will position himself in the temple of God, claiming that he himself is God. Don't you remember that I told you this when I was with you? And you know what is holding him back, for he can be revealed only when his time comes.

For this lawlessness is already at work secretly, and it will remain secret until the one who is holding it back steps out of the way. Then the man of lawlessness will be revealed, whom the Lord Jesus will consume with the breath of his mouth and destroy by the splendor of his coming. This evil man will come to do the work of Satan with counterfeit power and signs and miracles. He will use every kind of wicked deception to fool those who are on their way to destruction because they refuse to believe the truth that would save them. So God will send great deception upon them, and they will believe all these lies. Then they will be condemned for not believing the truth and for enjoying the evil they do.

As for us, we always thank God for you, dear brothers and sisters loved by the Lord. We are thankful that God chose you to be among the first to experience salvation, a salvation that came through the Spirit who makes you holy and by your belief in the truth. He called you to salvation when we told you the Good News; now you can share in the glory of our Lord Jesus Christ.

With all these things in mind, dear brothers and sisters, stand firm and keep a strong grip on everything we taught you both in person and by letter."

How are you spending your time as you wait for the return of Christ? Journal your thoughts today about this portion of scripture...are you waiting with stress in your life? Are you anticipating His return with excitement and hope? Waiting for the Lord to come should take on new meaning for us...maybe we need to really think about being part of building the Kingdom on a daily basis!

My Daily Journal

DAY 20

DAY 21

Savoring the moments...

People today have lost the ability to *savor*. Let me explain, Savoring. It is best described as one licking an ice cream cone. A forever lost in time experience...never once allowing it to drip through the bottom of the cone. It is getting all you can get out of the moment. It is being sure that you have licked every bit of the icing off of the beaters. Kids seem to be able to do this better than adults. I believe it is because adults are always rushing off to do something else.

My husband was stationed at Fort Ben-Harrison during the Korean Conflict. I would go with him to the train station and we would savor the moments by talking and listening, holding hands and being together. I would walk with him as far as I could to his train and place of departure...and then I would watch until the train moved out of the station and out into the night. I would take the bus home and remember all that we did and talked about in that brief but wonderful weekend.

Learning the importance of time and valuing it has great rewards. People who waste time will never complete the task. Savoring and enjoying the moments of our lives even in its smallest portions is a great gift. The small things are often more valuable than some huge event. Learning to discern what is the best and what is important will bring happiness to the person who has learned the difference. Spending time with grandparents can be a great reward for a child. Those who foolishly move forward without a plan will not find success. Savoring the Moments is not wasting time...it is valuing the gift of time and each day. It is developing those margins in our lives that will eventually balance out the entire day.

Proverbs 19:3
"People ruin their lives by their own foolishness and then are angry at the LORD."

Proverbs 19:20-21
"Get all the advice and instruction you can, and be wise the rest of your life. You can make many plans, but the LORD's purpose will prevail."

103

Proverbs 15:22
"Plans go wrong for lack of advice; many counselors bring success."

Making wise choices along the way can set the course for the rest of one's life. Learning to appreciate the little things and to enjoy simple things have great value. One person was asked, "If your house was on fire, what would you try to save as you ran out of the house?" The person replied, "The most valuable thing I have is my relationship with God, family, my friends, and memories."

What kind of memories are you making? A lot happens in one's life between birth and the grave! What you do in the "Living Time" says a lot about who you are and what you did and thought.

Proverbs 15:24
"The path of the wise leads to life above; they leave the grave behind."

Proverbs 15:31-33
"If you listen to constructive criticism, you will be at home among the wise. If you reject criticism, you only harm yourself; but if you listen to correction, you grow in understanding. Fear of the LORD teaches a person to be wise; humility precedes honor."

Life is made up of stages or cycles...the baby/child...the pre-teen and teen...the young adult and the adult. We move from these stages sometimes with great difficulty and the changes are not always easy to survive and master. How we live the moments are an indicator of how we will live our lives.

It is wonderful when we are given times to clear away the slate. I remember going from grade school to High School...it was a chance to leave the foolishness of a child behind and have a chance to be a new person. Going from High School to College was a huge leap...you could leave some of the old friends behind who might know your weaknesses and you could really make a fresh start. Isn't it strange how some of those negative behaviors follow us through each stage...to where we are presently? It is hard to throw off the acts of laziness and unprofitable thinking. Only in Christ can we be made new, "the old has passed away and everything has become new." I love it.

Christ is the one who gives us hope that we can learn from our mistakes and we can become new in our thinking and behaviors. You can develop the ability to embrace the moments. You can learn and grow in having an appreciation for the moments. We can risk, we can change, we can fail and we can grow. We can live as Forgiven People!

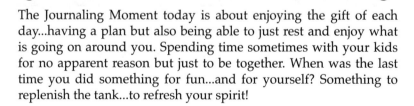

Ecclesiastes 3:1-13

"There is a time for everything, a season for every activity under heaven. A time to be born and a time to die. A time to plant and a time to harvest. A time to kill and a time to heal. A time to tear down and a time to rebuild. A time to cry and a time to laugh. A time to grieve and a time to dance. A time to scatter stones and a time to gather stones. A time to embrace and a time to turn away. A time to search and a time to lose. A time to keep and a time to throw away. A time to tear and a time to mend. A time to be quiet and a time to speak up. A time to love and a time to hate. A time for war and a time for peace.

What do people really get from all their hard work? I have thought about this in connection with the various kinds of work God has given people to do. God has made everything beautiful for its own time. He has planted eternity in the human heart, but even so, people cannot see the whole scope of God's work from beginning to end. So I concluded that there is nothing better for people than to be happy and to enjoy themselves as long as they can. And people should eat and drink and enjoy the fruits of their labor, for these are gifts from God."

The Journaling Moment today is about enjoying the gift of each day...having a plan but also being able to just rest and enjoy what is going on around you. Spending time sometimes with your kids for no apparent reason but just to be together. When was the last time you did something for fun...and for yourself? Something to replenish the tank...to refresh your spirit!

Let's have fun today...can be very rewarding...

Or...

Let's plan so we can have freedom...structure gives us a time for freedom...

We need margins...

Journal your fun times and memories of fun...along with seeing accomplishments as healthy and part of the plan God has for your life. He wants all of you...The Total Person has a balanced life.

BALANCE IS KEY!

My Daily
Journal

DAY
21

DAY 22

Interruptions are timely

I cannot believe how many times the phone rings when I am right in the middle of something very important. Can you imagine Jesus' life with a cell phone and a lap top? How we view interruptions is huge. They can be either God's appointments or they can cause us to be stressful. I have a list of things I want to get done during the day. I never allow for the phone calls...or for the things that the Lord may have on my daily list. I am starting to pray, "Whatever happens today, may I be open to understanding how this is your will for me." This little prayer has freed me up to accept whatever is happening and to trust in God's scheduling for my life.

Matthew 8:1-4
"Large crowds followed Jesus as he came down the mountainside. Suddenly, a man with leprosy approached Jesus. He knelt before him, worshiping. 'Lord,' the man said, 'if you want to, you can make me well again.'

Jesus touched him, 'I want to,' he said. 'Be healed!' And instantly the leprosy disappeared. Then Jesus said to him, 'Go right over to the priest and let him examine you. Don't talk to anyone along the way. Take along the offering required in the law of Moses for those who have been healed of leprosy, so everyone will have proof of your healing.'"

This interruption in the life of Jesus made all the difference in the world to this man...and to his family. He went from being an outcast to being able to return to the temple to worship. He was given the opportunity to have a job. Jesus, when he gets in your face...changes your whole life.

I have a friend who has recently accepted Christ and it has just been huge. His daughter accepted Christ and now his family is totally different from what it looked like a year ago.

The woman at the well in John chapter four was changed that day and her whole town was changed. The woman went out to get water at the well. It was midday...she was not the sort of woman who welcomed encounters with the other women in the community. She chose to go when others would not be there...and then she met Jesus. He asked her for a drink, and that was only the beginning. Her normal life as she knew it was interrupted and she had to come to grips with the sin factor in her life and her own unhappiness. She experienced an *interruption at the well...in the middle of the day.* She went to get a bucket of water and found the living water.

John 4:39-42
"Many Samaritans from the village believed in Jesus because the woman had said, 'He told me everything I ever did!' When they came out to see him, they begged him to stay at their village. So he stayed for two days, long enough for many of them to hear his message and believe. Then they said to the woman, 'Now we believe because we have heard him ourselves, not just because of what you told us. He is indeed the Savior of the world.'"

We have interruptions all the time...some of them are not interruptions we particularly enjoy. We face the unknown and wonder, why is this happening to us?

James 1:2-4
"Dear brothers and sisters, whenever trouble comes your way, let it be an opportunity for joy. For when your faith is tested, your endurance has a chance to grow. So let it grow, for when your endurance is fully developed, you will be strong in character and ready for anything."

So it is important to see the interruption as perhaps an opportunity for joy. Now isn't that a special way to view the will of God...and opportunity for joy!

James 4:13-17
"Look here, you people who say, 'Today or tomorrow we are going to a certain town and will stay there a year. We will do business there and make a profit.' How do you know what will happen tomorrow? For your life is like the morning fog—it's here a little while, then it's gone. What you ought to say is, 'If the Lord wants us to, we will live and do this or that.' Otherwise you will be boasting about your own plans, and all such boasting is evil. Remember, it is sin to know what you ought to do and then not do it."

The Lord willing...and the Lord's will.

Interruptions are opportunities that God may have placed in your life to encourage you in your walk with Him...or to strengthen you in your faith walk.

Today's Journaling Moment may have reminded you of the little people in your life who are constantly seeking and vying for your attention. They may seem like interruptions but they could also be opportunities to experience His joy. They ask so many questions and they need so much time. Their questions are often inappropriate and they take away from your time schedule.

There will come a day when you will want them to pick up the phone and give you a call...or you would love to be able to chat with them about anything...and the timing for that moment will be gone to you forever. Enjoy the little moments with them.

Reflect upon your interruptions today...as open doors.

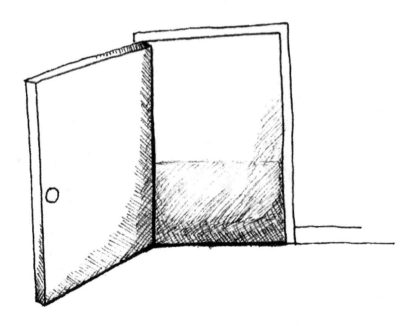

My Daily
Journal

DAY
22

DAY 23

Time Out!

Have you ever been caught in a situation that was so intense you just needed to take some *time out!* Getting away from the stress of the situation where you could once again focus...or get over your emotions from the constant bombardment of everything exploding in and around you!

If you have lived any length of time, I know you understand how getting away from the situation can be necessary and very healing. Children often need time out when they are getting on one another's nerves or they start to act more like children than you care to experience for the moment...and *time out* is needed to maintain your sense of well being and sanity as a parent. They are not terrible children just normal children who may need a nap.

But what happens when God decides to give us some *time out?*

I remember after my heart attack my Doctor telling me, "You need to take *some time out,* from your normal schedule and just get your strength back and take some Time Out to heal." Certainly not what I wanted to hear, but so necessary. It was so important to listen and follow instructions and take the time to rest, sleep, rest, reflect, observe...just relax! It was a long summer. I found it difficult to simply not have a plan...to just do whatever felt good to me that day. I kept telling myself this was his prescription and I should follow the Doctor's plan and just do it!

Ecclesiastes 5:19-20
"And it is a good thing to receive wealth from God and the good health to enjoy it. To enjoy your work and accept your lot in life–that is indeed a gift from God. People who do this rarely look with sorrow on the past, for God has given them reasons for joy."

It is hard to think of being set aside to wait for the Lord's leading in our lives. With a true sense of anticipation, we often find ourselves standing in the wings...waiting for the next scene...hoping we will soon get to perform our part. Why don't we want the director to tell us when it is time? Simply stated, we want to be in control

111

and in charge. We want life to be lived out according to our time frame...when we think it should be happening...and God says you are not quite ready for the next phase. We get anxious and we want to move before God's timing.

Isaiah 30:18
"But the LORD still waits for you to come to him so he can show you his love and compassion. For the LORD is a faithful God. Blessed are those who wait for him to help them."

Hurry up and Wait. We all know how to hurry...but learning to wait until God moves in our lives is a learning process. We need to wait sometimes for God to send us help and healing. I don't understand why this is so difficult...but I know learning total dependence upon the Lord is a life changing experience. We need reminders from time to time to just wait until the stress or pain goes away.

Sometimes we are given time out to regain a Godly perspective. We have been so beat up by the world's values we lose sight of the truth that will set us free.

Sometimes living with unconfessed sin in our lives causes us to be set aside until we are able to once again get a clear perspective of our situation and what needs to be our course. We cannot blindly follow along without having spiritual renewal in our hearts. We get worn down and our Christian values need to be revised.

A little boy was sitting in a chair. I asked him, "Are you waiting for someone?" He looked at me for a moment and replied, "No, I am waiting for my Mom to have a rest!" I don't know if they had been playing together or what had happened...but it struck me as being humorous. God doesn't need a rest from us...but he may need to allow us a time to think about our behaviors so we can choose to get back on course.

God made a huge promise to the Children of Israel, that he would never leave or forsake them. His promise conveyed his constant love for them. It was his covenant to them regarding his faithfulness and their concern for restoration, but they didn't believe his words and they choose often to do their own thing. Much like us today. God would then allow them to be carried away into captivity until they would once again cry out to God...in confession of their sin, asking for healing and restoration.

Time out can have a positive or a negative effect upon us, depending upon our attitude and how much we desire to be restored.

112

Colossians 3:12-15

"Since God chose you to be the holy people whom he loves, you must clothe yourselves with tenderhearted mercy, kindness, humility, gentleness, and patience. You must make allowance for each other's faults and forgive the person who offends you. Remember, the Lord forgave you, so you must forgive others. And the most important piece of clothing you must wear is love. Love is what binds us all together in perfect harmony. And let the peace that comes from Christ rule in your hearts. For as members of one body you are all called to live in peace. And always be thankful."

Today's Journaling Moment is focused on *Time Out*. You may be sitting this one out...you may feel that God has put you on hold. Perhaps, he is giving you time to reflect, repent, and release. The very purpose being his desire for you to have restoration either with him, or with someone else. Maybe you need to address the issue of why you have chosen your own self exile based upon your anger with the events in your life. Pause for a moment...Thank God for His goodness in your life and seek to complete the journey with the relationship restored.

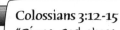

My Daily Journal

DAY

23

DAY 24

Time waits for no man!

I have heard this phrase since I was a small child. I could never really decide what it meant. I thought it meant, to hurry up or you will be left behind. Time doesn't wait for anyone...you can bank on that being true...but it may have several meanings. It depends on whose opinion you are listening to and who is quoting it to you.

I know the scripture talks about how waiting will bring some sort of virtue into your life and it is to be valued...but I often wonder, "What exactly am I waiting for?" Is the timing right?

God waits for man to come to the end of himself so he will finally come to Him, *but he doesn't wait forever.*

Isaiah 30:18
"But the LORD still waits for you to come to him so he can show you his love and compassion. For the LORD is a faithful God. Blessed are those who wait for him to help them."

Lamentations 3:22-27
"The unfailing love of the LORD never ends! By his mercies we have been kept from complete destruction. Great is his faithfulness; his mercies begin afresh each day. I say to myself, 'The LORD is my inheritance; therefore, I will hope in him!'

The LORD is wonderfully good to those who wait for him and seek him. So it is good to wait quietly for salvation from the LORD. And it is good for the young to submit to the yoke of his discipline."

Lamentations 3:31-33, 37-38
"For the Lord does not abandon anyone forever. Though he brings grief, he also shows compassion according to the greatness of his unfailing love. For he does not enjoy hurting people or causing them sorrow."

"Can anything happen without the Lord's permission? Is it not the Most High who helps one and harms another? Then why

115

should we, mere humans, complain when we are punished for our sins?"

This is an interesting grouping of scriptures. I read them and see the compassion and love of God in these verses but I also know that a day of reckoning is coming to those who have not yet put their trust and faith in Christ. I understand that time is running out and people do need to heed the call of the Holy Spirit to, "Come as they are." God so wants to rescue us from the destiny of hell which will be the reward of those who have not yet received forgiveness for sin.

Hebrews 3:12-19

"Be careful then, dear friends. Make sure that your own hearts are not evil and unbelieving, turning you away from the living God. You must warn each other every day, as long as it is called, 'today,' so that none of you will be deceived by sin and hardened against God. For if we are faithful to the end, trusting God just as firmly as when we first believed, we will share in all that belongs to Christ. But never forget the warning: 'Today you must listen to his voice. Don't harden your hearts against him as Israel did when they rebelled.'

And who were those people who rebelled against God, even though they heard his voice? Weren't they the ones Moses led out of Egypt? And who made God angry for forty years? Wasn't it the people who sinned, whose bodies fell in the wilderness? And to whom was God speaking when he vowed that they would never enter his place of rest? He was speaking to those who disobeyed him. So we see that they were not allowed to enter his rest because of their unbelief."

Hurry Up and Wait...in a sense this is the message. Accept Christ as your personal Savior today and be saved...and then Wait for His coming again. He is coming again to take all of us where he is and we will then enter into the perfect rest...being with Him forever.

We certainly do not want to be late for this great event. So, with the statement, Time waits for No Man...we can believe that it is true. Time is running out...we are not certain of the events that are starting to come into play. But we do know that in the last days, we will experience false teachers...and we are experiencing this now. We know that children will lose respect for parents and this is true for today, when they say, peace, peace...then sudden destruction will come upon them as a mother who is about to be delivered of a child.

I believe the events of today are serious enough for us to consider we are living in stressful times.

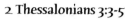

> **2 Thessalonians 3:3-5**
> "But the Lᴏʀᴅ is faithful; he will make you strong and guard you from the evil one. And we are confident in the Lᴏʀᴅ that you are practicing the things we commanded you, and that you always will. May the Lord bring you into an ever deeper understanding of the love of God and the endurance that comes from Christ."

We need to know that time doesn't wait...and the second coming of Christ will be right on time. Not too early, not too late...exactly when God says the timing is right. When the last person who is going to come into the kingdom makes his decision to accept Christ, He will return. The important question being, have you settled your sin problem...and received the Savior as your very own? Do you have a personal relationship with God the Father through his Son, Jesus?

In your Journal today consider the Mercy of God and ask yourself, what are you waiting to have happen in your life? Have you settled all of the important questions for yourself and has the Justice of God been satisfied by your decision to accept the provision of the cross for your sins?

My Daily Journal

DAY

24

DAY 25

Will you wait with me?

It is so much easier to go through life if someone is waiting with you! I have so appreciated over the years my family and friends who have chosen to wait with me. We know that many will rush with us and be hurried with us...but few will actually wait with us. It is such a needed thing in our lives to have someone to wait with us.

Waiting for children is hard...going through labor with us. It is wonderful when someone is willing to wait with you through the night or through the pain. Just to be there and maybe bring you a cup of coffee while you wait...not if you are in labor...but you can surely identify with this statement.

Jesus was preparing for the most crucial and difficult time of his life here on this earth. He had been praised in Jerusalem but now he was going to face his trial and his death on the cross. He asked the disciples to pray with him...to be with him as he waited for this time to pass. But they could not...they slept. They were so overcome with their own grief...they could only sleep.

Matthew 26:36-46
"Then Jesus brought them to an olive grove called Gethsemane, and he said, 'Sit here while I go on ahead to pray.' He took Peter and Zebedee's two sons, James and John, and he began to be filled with anguish and deep distress. He told them, 'My soul is crushed with grief to the point of death. Stay here and watch with me.'

He went a little farther and fell face down on the ground, praying, 'My Father! If it is possible, let this cup of suffering be taken away from me. Yet I want your will, not mine.' Then he returned to the disciples and found them asleep. He said to Peter, 'Couldn't you stay awake and watch with me even one hour? Keep alert and pray. Otherwise temptation will overpower you. For though the spirit is willing enough, the body is weak!'

Again he left them and prayed, 'My Father! If this cup cannot be taken away until I drink it, your will be done.' He returned

119

to them again and found them sleeping, for they just couldn't keep their eyes open.

So he went back to pray a third time, saying the same things again. Then he came to the disciples and said, 'Still sleeping? Still resting? Look, the time has come. I, the Son of Man, am betrayed into the hands of sinners. Up, let's be going. See, my betrayer is here!' "

Waiting with others as they go through difficult times takes energy and prayer. We simply cannot do it without prayer and we need others to be with us while we wait. Sometimes, the experiences we are going through seem so remote we want someone to validate what is happening to us and to perhaps acknowledge what we are seeing and feeling. It is not possible for people to fix us...we do know that, but having a friend to come along side and sit with us, makes the burden lighter.

A woman called one evening and related to me a tale of woe...it was such a pitiful story. I still do not know if all of the things she told me were true or not...but I had no way of getting to her or being where she was. I started to think how I could help. I made some suggestions for things she might do to receive some help in her situation. I listed them and then I finally realized...she had no energy. She was so overwhelmed with her situation.

All I could do was listen...and then pray with her! I could do nothing but listen and wait with her as she released her emotions and frustrations. I had no solutions or a quick prayer to offer her for the kind of help she was seeking.

Over and over again she thanked me for listening and praying for her. "You have been so kind, thank you! I can hear the kindness in your voice," she said. I hadn't really done much of anything but just listened. We chatted for over an hour. I had an appointment and so I told her, "I have to leave. I am so sorry. I will be praying for you." I suggested to her, "Go to my church in the morning and there will be some things there for you...and an envelope." It was all I could think to do. It was not fixing anything...it was doing what I could do.

I could not sleep very well that night. It was almost more than I could bear and I wondered how she could be living through such a terrible time in her life. How had all of these things happened in her life to bring her to this point, and why? We ask ourselves these questions when faced with problems that seemingly have no solutions...no quick fixes...we seem helpless and hopeless.

The next day I left some money at the church for her to pick up...and two bags of items I knew she needed and could use. I was just blown away by her circumstances...even as I prayed for her...I sensed in my own spirit a sense of helplessness. I could not imagine her fear and sense of loss.

I cannot imagine what Jesus faced on that night so long ago nor why the disciples could not wait and pray with him. But I know in this situation of modern day times...I was not able to do much. I prayed but I felt so weak and helpless. I knew that God would have to be the one who met her needs and frustrations. He was the hope we both needed. I was counting on my Heavenly Father to come to the rescue.

I often wonder what God does with the times we are asked to come along side of others and wait with them...and we can't. We fold...I have to leave it with Him. I can pray and do what I personally can, but I know for certain the Holy Spirit will come along and bring comfort and hope to anyone who needs Him. It is so easy to make a quick judgement about why and how that person got themselves into that particular situation...but really, we have no idea. We do not know what God is doing in their lives and we certainly cannot pass judgement upon them.

Pray today for your compassion to be real. Journal today about how God has sent people into your life, His care packages from God to us in our times of need. Often, they just wait with you and listen, thank Him for those people. Also, pray for those who have no one to wait with them. Ask God to provide help and hope for them in their times of despair. We are His!

My Daily Journal
DAY
25

DAY 26

Waiting for spring

I lived in Minnesota for twenty years and I can tell you...waiting for spring is a big deal up there! It is huge! The winter months seem like they stretch from October to April. Sometimes I thought for sure, spring would never come. I moved from a warmer climate where spring came early and we would find the hope of spring in a little crocus coming up in the later part of February. It was very different in Minnesota by comparison. The Minnesota winters were cold, long, and bleak, often you would not see the ground until much later in the year...some winters were not as drastic...but precious few!

Spring is such a time of Hope...and New Growth. It is a time for planting and looking forward to the future. The days get longer and God's Day Light Savings time comes into focus. After the short days of winter, I looked forward to the time when the daylight hours would be longer. I hated getting up in the dark, going to work in the dark and coming home in the dark. It seems like some of us do better when the daylight hours last for a longer period of time. I am one of those persons who loves the light.

Ecclesiastes 12:1-7
"Don't let the excitement of youth cause you to forget your Creator. Honor him in your youth before you grow old and no longer enjoy living. It will be too late then to remember him, when the light of the sun and moon and the stars is dim to your old eyes, and there is no silver lining left among the clouds. Your limbs will tremble with age, and your strong legs will grow weak. Your teeth will be too few to do their work, and you will be blind, too. And when your teeth are gone, keep your lips tightly closed when you eat! Even the chirping of birds will wake you up. But you yourself will be deaf and tuneless, with a quavering voice. You will be afraid of heights and of falling, white-haired and withered, dragging along without any sexual desire. You will be standing at death's door. And as you near your everlasting home, the mourners will walk along the streets.

Yes, remember your Creator now while you are young, before the silver cord of life snaps and the golden bowl is broken.

123

Don't wait until the water jar is smashed at the spring and the pulley is broken at the well. For then the dust will return to the earth, and the spirit will return to God who gave it."

"Remember the Creator of your youth while it is yet light." In our youth we just seem to ride along with our days quietly moving on. We think about time as passing so slowly. I remember at the age of sixteen thinking, *I'll never be old enough to drive and be on my own.* How foolish! All too quickly our lives come to the sunset times and we realize we have lived most of our lives and what in the world did we do and accomplish?

Every day is a gift. We can make some choices as to how we will live out those days.

Ecclesiastes 8:5-8
"Those who obey him will not be punished. Those who are wise will find a time and a way to do what is right. Yes, there is a time and a way for everything, even as people's troubles lie heavily upon them.

Indeed, how can people avoid what they don't know is going to happen? None of us can hold back our spirit from departing. None of us has the power to prevent the day of our death. There is no escaping that obligation, that dark battle. And in the face of death, wickedness will certainly not rescue those who practice it."

Our days are numbered...living each day looking for the Spring Time is not such a bad thing. However, how we make the application of what we are living through and experiencing to daily living is very important. Do we use the light to plant, to prepare for the summer? Do we make good use of the extra time? It is a choice! Living for the harvest means we have to prepare for the harvest.

Ephesians 3:14-21
"When I think of the wisdom and scope of God's plan, I fall to my knees and pray to the Father, the Creator of everything in heaven and on earth. I pray that from his glorious, unlimited resources he will give you mighty inner strength through his Holy Spirit. And I pray that Christ will be more and more at home in your hearts as you trust in him. May your roots go down deep into the soil of God's marvelous love. And may you have the power to understand, as all God's people should, how wide, how long, how high, and how deep his love really is.

May you experience the love of Christ, though it is so great you will never fully understand it. Then you will be filled with the fullness of life and power that comes from God.

Now glory be to God! By his mighty power at work within us, he is able to accomplish infinitely more than we would ever dare to ask or hope. May he be given glory in the church and in Christ Jesus forever and ever through endless ages. Amen."

Ephesians 4:30
"And do not bring sorrow to God's Holy Spirit by the way you live. Remember, he is the one who has identified you as his own, guaranteeing that you will be saved on the day of redemption."

Proverbs 13:9
"The life of the godly is full of light and joy, but the sinner's light is snuffed out."

Consider the seasons...Spring Time...and Fall. Each day in every season is a golden opportunity to live for Christ. To stand and be counted. A time to walk in the Spirit and to follow His leading while it is the day. We have so much happening in our world...we need to be diligent as we serve Him.

Journal today about your choices during all of the seasons. What choices are you facing? Look what happens, when you hurry!

My Daily Journal

DAY 26

DAY 27

Look what happens when you hurry

I have ruined more things in my life by hurrying and trying to make up for lost time. I remember ironing a blouse and hurrying...it looked terrible. Somewhere along the way, I learned, you cannot hurry good food. It takes time! A baked potato hurried is terrible, a hurried turkey is worse...and a hurried pie cannot be endured. A hurried pregnancy is a tragedy.

When you look seriously at life...it cannot be hurried! We have forgotten how to savor and enjoy the moments. I have slowed down and actually take the time to smell the roses. I stop and visit with my Mom even if it is just for a few moments. I cherish the moments with a dear friend. I linger over coffee with my daughter-in-love Dede...because I want to just enjoy the conversation and laugh together one more time. I want to visit with Glenda and find out how her day is going. I want to pray for the things that concern Lois. Value your relationships and cherish them...you cannot hurry friendships and relationships.

Galatians 6:3
"If you think you are too important to help someone in need, you are only fooling yourself. You are really a nobody."

Galatians 6:10
"Whenever we have the opportunity, we should do good to everyone, especially to our Christian brothers and sisters."

You cannot hurry your spiritual growth. It takes time. Time being in the word, praying and memorizing the word. You cannot grow your spiritual life without spending time in God's word being taught by the Holy Spirit.

Proverbs 15:14
"A wise person is hungry for truth, while the fool feeds on trash."

Proverbs 11:17
"Your own soul is nourished when you are kind, but you destroy yourself when you are cruel."

Proverbs 9:11-12
"Wisdom will multiply your days and add years to your life. If you become wise, you will be the one to benefit. If you scorn wisdom, you will be the one to suffer."

We often run from the discipline of time. We cannot hurry through our lives without reaping the results. We must learn to deal with patience and taking time to do something right the first time rather than having to repeat the process again. Failure becomes our teacher and if we learn positive lessons from the experience, we have redeemed the time. Making poor decisions, trying to skip part of the process is not always a good teacher, but if we allow God to show us, we can even learn from the times when we have hurried through the process and missed the main truth. I have been there!

Proverbs 1:7
"Fear of the LORD is the beginning of knowledge. Only fools despise wisdom and discipline."

Proverbs 15:33
"Fear of the LORD teaches a person to be wise; humility precedes honor."

If you are busy trying to hurry up your life and moving rather quickly through the process...remember the great little saying we learned in Kindergarten, STOP...LOOK...AND LISTEN! The lesson we learned from our parents and our teachers in reference to crossing the street is still a good lesson for us today as far as our spiritual growth is concerned.

We hurry through so much of life. We rush, we even run...we try so desperately to catch up and make up for lost time...or we keep trying to make up for the time which has passed us by. We go backwards rather than moving forward. The past serves a purpose...we learn from our mistakes and we learn from the past. We must allow God to heal the pain of failure and the past, as we step into the present and the future.

Proverbs 15:22
"Plans go wrong for lack of advice; many counselors bring success."

Proverbs 15:32
"If you reject criticism, you will only harm yourself; but if you listen to correction, you grow in understanding."

> **Ecclesiastes 5:19-20**
> "And it is a good thing to receive wealth from God and the good health to enjoy it. To enjoy your work and accept your lot in life–that is indeed a gift from God. People who do this rarely look with sorrow on the past, for God has given them a reason for joy."

The words for today in your Journal should focus upon the things you have tried to hurry...and they failed. But rejoice in the fact that God knows all about it...and He is giving you new opportunities to take the time needed. It is not about perfection...but learning to walk in His wisdom and be wise in your choices knowing that He will get you through whatever needs to happen. Ask God to show you in a clear way the things you can change...and then move forward with confidence believing He has erased the past and you have a new slate. Start the process...with consideration of giving God the time He needs to work in your life on a daily basis.

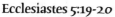

My Daily Journal

DAY

27

DAY 28

We're waiting to have children

My friend and I were talking about her niece and how they were expecting. They have only been married a little over a year. "It was kind of unexpected but now that they are pregnant, they can see it as a good thing." That is one response to having children. Others feel they should wait and be more prepared. Marilyn and I commented how babies just have a way of showing up and you can make out of it what you want. If you plan, it can seem at times that you will never be prepared or totally ready. Some couples purposely wait and they plan every minute detail. Others wait and a baby never comes. When is the waiting enough?

Barrenness is such a hard issue to deal with if you really want a child. It seems like everyone you meet on the streets is pregnant. It seems like all of your friends have children everywhere and when you don't have any or you only have one, it can become a huge focus in your life. Children are such a blessing and an extension of you as parents.

God had such a perfect plan for his creation to reproduce. Having the human race enter the world as little babies is such a beautiful thing. No one who has experienced giving birth can deny how beautiful and special it really is. Children do bring us into a special relationship with our Heavenly Father. I remember looking at my first born son, Michael, and just being so impressed with the miracle of birth and how God was in the midst of the whole experience. I have never experienced anything like it before. Being born into His Kingdom is also one of those times when you know it is beyond your own understanding and human terms cannot describe what is happening.

Young people today tell me, "We are waiting to have children." I am sure they have reasons and they have thought about the economic situation in their lives and in our world. They are also afraid to bring children into the world today because we are living in perilous times. These are very real issues for them and they must consider the plan and purpose of God in their lives. I do not have an answer as to right or wrong...I am only saying, more families are being delayed for one reason or another. Getting married later in life

131

is another option some are making and that definitely plays a part in the decision making process.

I am sad when they have waited too long...and it never happens, or there may be a physical problem and conceiving and giving birth is not possible. Sarah in the Old Testament faced some of these issues. She wanted more than anything to have a child. She waited and waited...and her clock had definitely run out. Her option was to run ahead of God and she came up with her own plan. She involved her hand maiden, Hagar, and asked her husband to sleep with her and have a child with Hagar.

It was evident after the birth of Hagar's child, Ishmael, that the problem was with Sarah not Abraham. It was Sarah who was barren. Such a difficult thing to deal with in those days...when having children gave a woman a sense of worth and well being. I don't totally understand the rationale of everything that happened in this real situation but in reading the scripture many things come to light.

Galatians 4:21-31
"Listen to me, you who want to live under the law. Do you know what the law really says? The Scriptures say that Abraham had two sons, one from his slave-wife and one from his freeborn wife. The son of the slave-wife was born in a human attempt to bring about the fulfillment of God's promise. But the son of the freeborn wife was born as God's own fulfillment of his promise.

Now these two women serve as an illustration of God's two covenants. Hagar, the slave-wife, represents Mount Sinai where people first became enslaved to the law. And now Jerusalem is just like Mount Sinai in Arabia, because she and her children live in slavery. But Sarah, the free woman, represents the heavenly Jerusalem. And she is our mother. That is what Isaiah meant when he prophesied,

'Rejoice, O childless woman! Break forth into loud and joyful song, even though you never gave birth to a child. For the woman who could bear no children now has more than all the other women!'

And you, dear brothers and sisters, are children of the promise, just like Isaac. And we who are born of the Holy Spirit are persecuted by those who want us to keep the law, just as Isaac, the child of promise, was persecuted by Ishmael, the son of the slave-wife.

But what do the Scriptures say about that? 'Get rid of the slave and her son, for the son of the slave woman will not share the family inheritance with the free woman's son.' So, dear friends, we are not children of the slave woman, obligated to the law. We are children of the free woman, acceptable to God because of our faith."

Galatians 5:1
"So Christ has really set us free. Now make sure that you stay free, and don't get tied up again in slavery to the law."

Interesting lesson we learn from the common occurrence in dealing with children and the importance of children in our lives. God used this situation to teach us a very important lesson. We need to believe that every circumstance in our lives has some meaning and purpose.

If you have children...you are blessed. If not, you are blessed. Not in the same way, but God does have a purpose in what is happening in your life. I am so thankful for women who find the strength to give up a child...to be free enough to release that child to go to another home where loving parents can care for the child and provide for the child as their own. This kind of love is beyond my own comprehension. I am respectful of people who are called to obey this command in their lives. It is a great cost to them emotionally and personally. I am also respectful of those who will adopt and care for those children as their own flesh and blood.

Jesus loved little children...and placed a high value upon them.

Mark 10:16
"Then he took the children into his arms and placed his hands on their heads and blessed them."

Jesus always wanted to honor little children. The disciples thought he would be disturbed by them but he brought them center stage and gave us the example of their importance in this portion of scripture. Women and children have always been respected by Jesus. He makes a difference in the lives of women in our world today. Women and children were always honored and widows were also treated with respect.

Isaiah 59:21 tells us that God's Spirit will pursue your children. Please read it in your bible.

There is no greater joy in the life of a parent or grandparent than to see our children walking in fellowship with the Lord.

This Sunday I am going to the baptismal service of two of my grandchildren, Jonathan, 17...and Natalie, 13. I count it a privilege to be there and to experience this special time with them and their family. The Lord is pleased as well.

If you are waiting for children...I pray your time of waiting will be honored. When Sarah heard that she was indeed going to bear a child in her old age...she laughed. It seems like a normal response to me. I think she was overjoyed and overwhelmed to believe it was still possible with God. Elizabeth in the New Testament was an encouragement to the mother of Jesus. "The one who was barren is now with child," this is what the angel told Mary to give her hope that she would and could bare a child. "Nothing is impossible with God."

Journal today and thank the Lord for the children in your midst. Pray for those children who have not been treated with respect in many parts of the world because of the greed and violence brought on by others. Ask God to remind you of the children who are homeless and without hope.

Write a prayer today for those children and then for those children who you know who are blessed. Be encouraged. We know God hears our prayers.

Jesus loves the little children...all the children of the world. Red and yellow, black and white, they are precious in His sight...Jesus loves the little children of the world.

My Daily Journal

DAY

28

DAY 29

The waiting room

If you have ever sat in a *waiting room*...you know it is a place where you are not in charge. You are waiting for someone to come out of surgery, you are waiting for a baby to be born, you are waiting for something to be accomplished beyond your expertise. Waiting for the dentist...waiting to see or hear about a situation beyond your own abilities.

Waiting Rooms...are not always waiting for surgery. I had to wait for new tires to be put on my car the other day. The room contained a television, magazines and comfortable chairs...it was a plain room with no windows and it served the purpose. A place for the customer to wait while being served. *Waiting rooms serve a purpose.* They are a place for one to wait while something you are waiting for is being serviced or until the people you are waiting to see can accommodate you.

One of the most painful places I ever waited was in a *waiting room in Milwaukee...waiting for my husband to have by-pass surgery.* He had the surgery, but they could not complete it because his chest cavity was full of infection and they could not do the heart surgery. The doctor placed him on huge dosages of antibiotics hoping it would clear up the infection before he had to have the surgery but before the surgery was scheduled again, he went into cardiac arrest. They were forced to do the surgery. It was a total success, seven by-pass surgery, but the infection killed him two weeks later. We just never know, do we? Waiting for our lives to change and be different is a difficult and growing process.

Joshua took over the leadership of the children of Israel. He stepped into the position of leadership feeling somewhat insecure, he was chosen by God but he didn't feel quite ready for the challenge. He had observed all that God had done for the children of Israel and for Moses, their leader. He was standing in the wings...he was observing all God had been doing for Moses and the children of Israel but he was viewing the situation from the safety of the *waiting room.*

God's words to Joshua were loud and clear.

Joshua 1:9

"Be strong and courageous! Do not be afraid or discouraged. For the Lord your God is with you wherever you go."

Over and over Joshua received encouragement and instructions for the next step in his journey of walking with God. Joshua was to learn about God firsthand...as His protector and leader. God was in charge and He kept taking Joshua to the next level of obedience and commitment.

Joshua 11:15

"As the LORD had commanded his servant Moses, so Moses commanded Joshua. And Joshua did as he was told, carefully obeying all of the LORD's instructions to Moses."

We have a lot of time to think while we are waiting in the LORD's *waiting room*. We have time to watch television, read a magazine, listen to the conversations of others, play games with our children, or just sit, wait and pray...and perhaps, stare out the window, if there is one. We use the time in the *waiting room* for a time of rest, asking God to give us peace in the midst of our anxious thoughts...sometimes just being quiet praying. We choose what our experience will be.

Joshua had completed the task...he had followed the course set before him and he had a few closing remarks to make. He said them very clearly and direct.

Joshua 23:14-16

"Soon I will die, going the way of all the earth. Deep in your hearts you know that every promise of the LORD your God has come true. Not a single one has failed! But as surely as the LORD your God has given you the good things he promised, he will also bring disaster on you if you disobey him. He will completely wipe you out from this good land he has given you. If you break the covenant of the LORD your God by worshiping and serving other gods, his anger will burn against you, and you will quickly be wiped out from the good land he has given you."

He had learned well the lessons so clearly taught in the *waiting room*. Joshua had stepped up to the plate and he was counted. He took on the role of being very responsible and accountable. He could not be Moses...he could only be himself. He was encouraged and comforted by God to go beyond himself and to obediently follow the Lord's directions for himself and for the children of Israel.

138

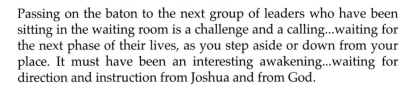

Joshua 23:6-8

"So be strong! Be very careful to follow all the instructions written in the Book of the Law of Moses. Do not deviate from them in any way. Make sure you do not associate with the other people still remaining in the land. Do not even mention the names of their gods, much less swear by them or worship them. But be faithful to the LORD your God as you have done until now."

Passing on the baton to the next group of leaders who have been sitting in the waiting room is a challenge and a calling...waiting for the next phase of their lives, as you step aside or down from your place. It must have been an interesting awakening...waiting for direction and instruction from Joshua and from God.

Today, you may feel like you are just hanging out and waiting in a room. You are not clear where God is taking you or what you should be learning...you are merely waiting for your instructions and someone to tell you the next step. Journal today, how you are feeling as you are waiting to step up and maybe you are wondering, "What is God going to do with me next?" As you wait, listen and be willing to obey every word of instructions. His promises are true and He is a faithful God.

You may be the one who has been the leader...and now you must step aside...do it graciously.

My Daily Journal

DAY

29

DAY 30

Day by day and with each passing moment

These familiar words from an old Swedish Hymn have caused me to think in terms of the reality of time and waiting. The words go on to say:

> "Day by Day and with each passing moment, strength I find to meet my trials here.
> Trusting in my Father's wise bestowment, I have no cause for worry or for fear.
> He whose heart is kind beyond all measure gives unto each day what He deems best.
> Lovingly, it's part of pain and pleasure...mingling toil with peace and rest."

Daily we have to live out our lives as we walk by faith and not by sight. I think if we knew what the course of a certain day would bring, we would surely stay in bed...or just check the day off: *Not participating today!* I am sure if people could have known the events of 911...they would have chosen to stay home on that day.

We simply do not know the events of each day and how they will effect our lives or the lives of those we hold dear.

We don't know what a day will bring. We cannot put off giving our hearts and lives to Christ, hoping that we can make that choice when we are ready. Giving up our sin to have eternal life is not a choice we want to put off.

Hebrews 3:7b-8a
"Today you must listen to his voice. Do not harden your hearts against him."

Aren't you glad God has chosen to share the gospel with all of us...giving us opportunity to hear and receive the message of truth. Jesus came to seek and to save sinners! What a marvelous truth to behold. The Gospel of Christ is the highest blessing to give and the greatest blessing to receive.

141

Psalm 17:7-8

"Show me your unfailing love in wonderful ways. You save with your strength those who seek refuge from their enemies.

Guard me as the apple of your eye. Hide me in the shadow of your wings."

Our days are truly numbered. Where else can we go, eternal life comes only through knowing the Son.

1 John 5:11-12
"And this is what God has testified: He has given us eternal life, and this life is in his Son. So whoever has God's Son has life; whoever does not have his Son does not have life."

The first need we have in the midst of our thoughts about the days and moments of our lives is to be saved and come into His Kingdom.

2 Peter 3:8-18

"But you must not forget, dear friends, that a day is like a thousand years to the Lord, and a thousand years is like a day. The Lord isn't really being slow about his promise to return, as some people think. No, he is being patient for your sake. He does not want anyone to perish, so he is giving more time for everyone to repent. But the day of the Lord will come as unexpectedly as a thief. Then the heavens will pass away with a terrible noise, and everything in them will disappear in fire, and the earth and everything on it will be exposed to judgment.

Since everything around us is going to melt away, what holy, godly lives you should be living! You should look forward to that day and hurry it along–the day when God will set the heavens on fire and the elements will melt away in the flames. But we are looking forward to the new heavens and new earth he has promised, a world where everyone is right with God.

And so, dear friends, while you are waiting for these things to happen, make every effort to live a pure and blameless life. And be at peace with God.

And remember, the Lord is waiting so that people have time to be saved. This is just as our beloved brother Paul wrote to you with the wisdom God gave him–speaking of these things in all of his letters. Some of his comments are hard to understand, and those who are ignorant and unstable have twisted his letters around to mean something quite different from what he meant, just as they do the other parts of Scripture–and the result is disaster for them.

I am warning you ahead of time, dear friends, so that you can watch out and not be carried away by the errors of these wicked people. I don't want you to lose your own secure footing. But grow in the special favor and knowledge of our Lord and Savior Jesus Christ.

To him be all glory and honor, both now and forevermore. Amen."

The second concept we need to ponder and be assured of in our thinking is to know He cares for us daily and He will be our resource in the times of stress and confusion. We can count on it!

The third thing we must consider is looking forward to the second coming of Christ. He is coming again and we should number our days with this thought clearly imprinted in our minds. If we belong to Him, we can count on the fact, He will come again. He said He would return...and He keeps all of His promises to His children.

Each day has its challenges and its moments. We can learn to walk with integrity and with confidence as we wait for the fulfillment of His second coming. He is coming again...for those who have accepted Him and for those who have not. He is coming again. I would hope and pray you have settled the question of where you are personally with the Lord. Do you know Him? If you have answered that question, then you can answer the next question, because of what Christ has done for all of us the problem of sin is settled. Christ satisfied the justice of God and we can look forward to His coming again.

Journal your thoughts today considering how you might be feeling about Christ coming again. Even though you may be ready, you may want to pray for others to come along side of you in this waiting process. We are ready and we want others to join us. It will be a time of reconciliation and reckoning.

My Daily Journal

DAY
30

DAY 31

Anticipation and blessings

I always enjoy a good meal...but I also look forward to, "What's for Dessert?" As a child, I started waiting for Christmas in September and I was really ready by Thanksgiving. We are always anticipating the future, an event...a happening, a blessing! We look toward the future and what is before us with great expectations. We start thinking about the benefits or the rewards with excitement and giddiness with our childlike spirits, the concept of *Hurry Up And Wait takes over and we are useless.* Parents often make the mistake of telling little children about the upcoming event of a new baby brother or sister too soon. Then the little children ask everyday, is this the day we are going to get our new baby? You learn after awhile not to give children too much information because they simply do not have the gift of "waiting"...and we do!

Part of learning to walk by faith and not by sight is trusting God to be in control of every situation. He does have a plan and a purpose for our lives. The Lord has rewards for those who trust in Him and look to Him for guidance and substance. He absolutely does want to bless His children with good things.

> **Psalm 25:8-10**
> "The LORD is good and does what is right; he shows the proper path to those who go astray. He leads the humble in what is right, teaching them his way. The LORD leads with unfailing love and faithfulness all those who keep his covenant and obey his decrees."

When we walk with the Lord we know there are consequences and rewards. The bottom line is cause and effect. If we do this, God will do this...it seems like a strange equation to me, without the mercy of God in my life, I know I could not survive nor would there be any hope or anticipation in my life.

God wants to bless us on a daily basis: Blessings are from God based upon our relationship with him through his son, Jesus...our Savior...our Hope for the future.

Jeremiah 17:7
"But blessed are those who trust in the LORD and have made the LORD their hope and confidence."

Psalm 84:11-12
"For the LORD God is our light and protector. He gives us grace and glory. No good thing will the LORD withhold from those who do what is right. O LORD Almighty, happy are those who trust in you."

When we come to know the Lord Jesus as our personal Savior we have no clue as to what is in our future. We don't know what is in store. Jesus has some encouraging words for his disciples, but they were not fully aware of what he meant regarding their future. We read the scriptures now and understand so many more things but the disciples were hearing these promises for the first time.

John 14:1-7
"Don't be troubled. You trust God, now trust in me. There are many rooms in my Father's home, and I am going to prepare a place for you. If this were not so, I would tell you plainly. When everything is ready, I will come and get you, so that you will always be with me where I am. And you know where I am going and how to get there."

"No we don't know, Lord," Thomas said. "We haven't any idea where you are going, so how can we know the way?"

Jesus told him, "I am the way, the truth, and the life. No one can come to the Father except through me. If you had known who I am, then you would have known who my Father is. From now on you know him and have seen him!"

I am thinking about how exciting it is going to be to see the actual place Jesus, the carpenter and the creator of the universe, is preparing for me. He made the heavens and the earth and the rest of the world in six days...what is heaven going to be like? I know it is far beyond what I can imagine or think. I know it will exceed all of my expectations because my small brain cannot comprehend the majesty of what that "place," is going to be like. I am excited to think about living there!

Heaven, for the most part is not a place we are anxious to go. When we are ready and when those numbered days have passed we will be ready. Many times my Mom, who is 92, says she is ready to go home and each day she thinks about the prospect of heaven and what it will actually be like. The other day she commented, ever so calmly, "I hope my sisters haven't been having all the fun!"

Anticipation and Blessings...promises not yet redeemed!

In the meantime, while we are waiting...Jesus promised not to leave us without a comforter and without a presence of His Spirit...the Holy Spirit. He will come along side of us and be with us while we are waiting and thinking about the future.

He has also left us here to do the work of bringing others into the Kingdom.

John 14:12-14
"The truth is, anyone who believes in me will do the same works I have done, and even greater works, because I am going to be with the Father. You can ask for anything in my name, and I will do it, because the work of the Son brings glory to the Father. Yes, ask anything in my name, and I will do it!"

A powerful concept. Today, as you Journal focus on the anticipation and the blessings of knowing Christ and the possibilities of what that concept means to you on a human level. Pray and ask God to reveal your work...and your part in building the Kingdom. Maybe you have already thought of some of those things...and you are doing them. Thank Him for the privilege of serving as you wait.

The idea of waiting can be frustrating but when you think of all we have to do...we need to be busy until the time is all used up.

John 14:30-31
"I don't have much more time to talk to you, because the prince of this world approaches. He has no power over me, but I will do what the Father requires of me, so that the world will know that I love the Father. Come, let's be going."

Carry on...

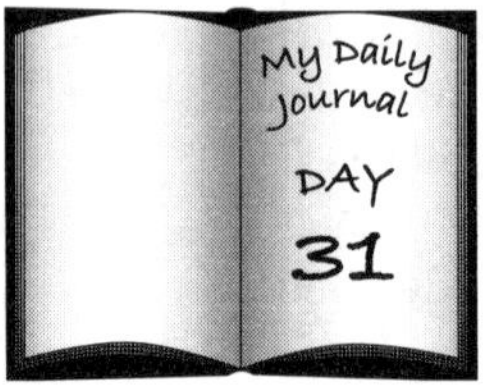
My Daily Journal
DAY
31

Priorities and planning still require waiting

DAY 32

I don't care how well you plan and what priorities you set down for yourself, there will be times when you will be required to wait. My Mom needed a new roof for her house. I called the insurance company...the insurance adjuster had to come out and check the damage. Another person had to come and give an estimate...then we had to get another estimate. The insurance adjuster had to send out the estimate. I had to contact the actual person to do the job. We were then placed on a waiting list...and three months later, we still do not have the roof replaced or the damage in the bathroom repaired. The roof is in the process of being put on, but I ask myself, what has all the business of priorities and planning to do with getting it done? My husband used to take care of these kinds of emergencies and situations. I don't recall he had all of these problems...perhaps, it was because I was not involved!

I hate to think of what the situation would be without any plans or any priorities. I cannot imagine my life on a daily basis without some kind of plan being put into motion. I have little lists and I do the lists. It isn't about forgetting the things on the list...it is about having a sense of accomplishment when something finally does get done. A lot of time is spent waiting...waiting for others to act on our behalf or waiting until the timing is finalized and we can enjoy the finished product.

I know that God is a planner and he probably has priorities. This of course is said, with tongue in cheek. I cannot imagine how he keeps track of all of us...and thinks of all of us individually as being important and special. I recently was doing child care with two-and three-year-olds. I decided we would serve tea in our pretend world, immediately they were all over me...in my lap, moving their chairs as close as they could. They all wanted individual attention and I didn't have enough room on my lap for all of them...or a sufficient number of arms and hands to hold them and meet their needs. We finally came to the conclusion, *we would have to take turns*. It was a simple solution to an overwhelming task.

As I think of these simple illustrations I understand the process of waiting and taking my turn. I cannot expect my life to be followed up by the God of the Universe instantly. Sometimes his response to my life situation has been, *for now, you will have to be put on hold.* It doesn't make me any more patient as I wait, but it does give me a human concept of how I am waiting for my turn. It gives me a way of relating to God with my simple human terms. I can grasp the concept of not getting what I want when I want it. I realize I must wait for my turn. Others are involved in the plan and in the priorities. We often forget we are not the only ones involved. My obedience is important...and often the obedience and disobedience of others will effect me.

Ecclesiastes 6:10
"Everything has already been decided. It was known long ago what each person would be. So there's no use arguing with God about your destiny."

Doesn't that nail a lot of things down when we start complaining about who we are and what is happening in our lives. Does that mean we can't change or grow or become something different? NO...it means, that God knows who we are, what we will do and how we will do it. Scary!

Ecclesiastes 7:8
"Finishing is better than starting. Patience is better than pride."

Ecclesiastes 7:10
"Don't long for "the good old days," for you don't know whether they were any better than today."

Ecclesiastes 8:16-17
"In my search for wisdom, I tried to observe everything that goes on all across the earth. I discovered that there is a ceaseless activity, day and night. This reminded me that no one can discover everything God has created in our world, no matter how hard they work at it. Not even the wisest people know everything, even if they say they do."

God will be with us during all of our times. He is waiting with us and He is walking with us through the times when we are feeling useless and afraid and not sure of our next move.

Isaiah 46:4
"I will be your God throughout your lifetime–until your hair is

white with age. I made you, and I will care for you. I will carry you along and save you."

Isaiah 46:10
"Only I can tell you what is going to happen even before it happens. Everything I plan will come to pass, for I do whatever I wish."

I have to remind myself of these verses over and over again. I cannot hear them enough. I am in the process of learning to trust God during the waiting times and seeing this time as a gift of mercy and grace. It is learning about the faith walk. It is walking with God not by what I can see or predict or observe. It is trusting and believing that He is constantly with me...watching over me and caring for me during all of my times. We are His!

The plans of God will come to pass. God is not slack concerning any of his promises toward his children. We can count on His faithfulness even when we are faithless.

In the year of 1999, I had a major heart attack and the verse the Lord had given me for that year in December of 1998 was a powerful verse. I clung to this verse and it gave me hope in the midst of my physical testing. I kept trying to believe that I would once again be healthy and I could live my little life as I knew it. My health issues were important for me and God assured me...in December before my heart attack in April...I would be fine! Not perfect...but fine!

Isaiah 58:11
"The LORD will guide you continually, watering your life when you are dry and keeping you healthy, too. You will be like a well-watered garden, like an ever-flowing spring."

I often wish I could know the plans and purposes of God. I want to understand my life based upon what His priorities are for me...but then I would not have to trust and follow based upon faith. I would be walking by sight and it would not be a matter of really having to trust in the midst of the darkness...waiting for my turn and waiting for more light on the path.

Jeremiah seemed to understand his calling in life from a very young age. He understood his purpose and he knew from the Lord his destiny. Most of us, flounder and live out our lives in stages.

151

Jeremiah 1:4-8

"The LORD gave me a message. He said, 'I knew you before I formed you in your mother's womb. Before you were born I set you apart and appointed you as my spokesman to the world.'

'O Sovereign LORD,' I said, 'I can't speak for you! I'm too young!'

'Don't say that,' the LORD replied, 'for you must go wherever I send you and say whatever I tell you. And don't be afraid of the people, for I will be with you and take care of you. I, the LORD, have spoken!'"

Jeremiah had a very difficult task...but he was constantly reminded that the LORD would be with him caring for him and directing his steps. The children of Israel did not want any part of the message God had commissioned him to speak. They did not want to hear his message of repentance. He was faithful, he delivered the truth and was often rejected. I am sure it was helpful to Jeremiah to know what his purpose was and why he needed to follow God rather than be praised and accepted by men.

As you journal today, look at your life. Does it feel like you are waiting for your turn? Are you assured of God's faithfulness in your life? He has a plan and a purpose for your life. He is clearing out the path so you can walk on it. Thank Him today for being with you and guiding you thus far...ask Him for the next set of directions and then walk in the Spirit as you serve Him daily.

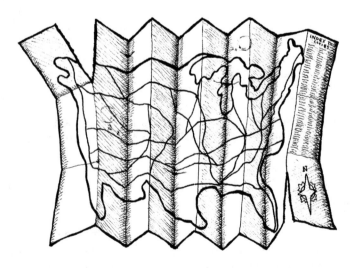

My Daily
Journal

DAY
32

DAY 33

But the time is coming!

We have been learning in our Singles Group about the true meaning of worship. We have been looking at how God is calling us to find meaning and purpose for our lives. One way of finding our meaning and purpose is to glorify God in and through our worship of Him. It has caused me to view worship in a new light...one of enjoyment while focusing upon the character of the Almighty God! I am worshiping God by just being me.

> **John 4:21-24**
> "Jesus replied, 'Believe me, the time is coming when it will no longer matter whether you worship the Father here or in Jerusalem. You Samaritans know so little about the one you worship, while we Jews know all about him, for salvation comes through the Jews. But the time is coming and is already here when true worshipers will worship the Father in spirit and in truth. The Father is looking for anyone who will worship him that way. For God is Spirit, so those who worship him must worship in spirit and in truth.'"

Jesus had been speaking to the woman at the well...and she brought up the issue of worship along with other concerns she had. She was trying to let Jesus know that even though she wasn't a perfect person, she did know something about spiritual matters. She was trying to convey her heart. She might be living the kind of life she was living but she was still interested in her spirituality. She had no idea of how her life was about to change.

I meet people today who are going to worship and they express concerns about religious points of view...while running from the main thing.

Who indeed are we worshiping and who are we serving?

It is not about going to church and attending services or worshiping God. God is concerned about the question of where He is in their hearts. He wants to know if we know HIM? Do we know Him based upon personally knowing His Son! We cannot truly Worship God without having this personal living relationship with His Son.

155

John 4:25-26

"The woman said, 'I know the Messiah will come–the one who is called Christ. When he comes, he will explain everything to us.'

Then Jesus told her, 'I am the Messiah!' "

Jesus has indeed come, and if we intend to truly worship the Father, we must come by the way of the cross and through his Son.

John 5:24-30

"I assure you, those who listen to my message and believe in God who sent me have eternal life. They will never be condemned for their sins, but they have already passed from death into life. And I assure you that the time is coming, in fact it is here, when the dead will hear my voice–the voice of the Son of God. And those who listen will live. The Father has life in himself, and he has granted his Son to have life in himself. And he has given him authority to judge all mankind because he is the Son of Man. Don't be so surprised! Indeed, the time is coming when all the dead in their graves will hear the voice of God's Son, and they will rise again. Those who have done good will rise to eternal life, and those who have continued in evil will rise to judgment. But I do nothing without consulting the Father. I judge as I am told. And my judgment is absolutely just, because it is according to the will of God who sent me; it is not merely my own."

John 14:6

"Jesus told him, 'I am the way, the truth, and the life. No one can come to the Father accept through me.' "

We may be religious and think we are truly worshiping God...but the only kind of worship God the Father can accept is when it comes from one who has been given new life. When the issues of sin have been wiped away by the blood of Christ...then we can truly be free to worship in spirit and in truth. He died for our sins. He gave His life to satisfy the justice of God. We need to believe in Jesus Christ for He alone can bring us into a right relationship with the Father. When our sins are forgiven...we have peace with God.

Yes, the day is coming...

Hebrews 3:12-15

"Be careful then, dear friends. Make sure that your own hearts are not evil and unbelieving, turning you away from the living God. You must warn each other every day, as long as it is called 'today,' so that none of you will be deceived by sin and hardened against God. For if we are faithful to the end, trusting God just as firmly as when we first believed, we will share in all that belongs to Christ. But never forget the warning: 'Today you must listen to his voice. Don't harden your hearts against him as Israel did when they rebelled.'"

The woman came to the well that day many years ago, expecting to fill her pots with water. She would learn about Jesus and experience the LIVING WATER. Once she accepted His provision for her sins...she would never thirst again...the questions of her spiritually were forever settled.

Hebrews 3:7b-8a
"Today, you must listen to his voice. Don't harden your hearts against him."

John 14:28-29
"Remember what I told you: I am going away, but I will come back to you again. If you really love me, you will be very happy for me, because now I can go to the Father, who is greater than I am. I have told you these things before they happen so that you will believe when they do happen."

Jesus has gone back to the Father...but He is coming again. On that day when Christ returns, I pray you will be ready to join Him in the sky.

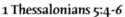

1 Thessalonians 5:4-6
"But you aren't in the dark about these things, dear brothers and sisters, and you won't be surprised when the day of the Lord comes like a thief. For you are all children of the light and of the day; we don't belong to darkness and night. So be on your guard, not asleep like the others. Stay alert and be sober."

Journaling today is a reminder, to remember each day brings us closer to the day when He will return. Pray for those around you who are not saved...not alert...not watching. Pray for yourself to be watching and waiting. Write your thoughts today about what it means to you to be ready to Worship God the Father...and to be in His presence forever.

My Daily Journal

DAY

33

DAY 34

Forty days of testing...forty years of testing!

We know about the testing of Jesus in the wilderness for forty days. Satan, himself was trying to tempt Jesus, taking him through a terrible time of testing just after his baptism...after being affirmed by the Father. So many times after we have been affirmed by the Father or we have had a time of spiritual renewal the enemy will come to us with doubts and temptations.

Luke 3:21-22
"One day when the crowds were being baptized, Jesus himself was baptized. As he was praying, the heavens opened, and the Holy Spirit descended on him in the form of a dove. And a voice from heaven said, 'You are my beloved Son, and I am fully pleased with you.'"

The enemy Satan...the enemy of us all...came along and took Jesus on a field trip. He is constantly trying to disrupt us in our faith walk.

Luke 4:1-13
"Then Jesus, full of the Holy Spirit, left the Jordan River. He was led by the Spirit to go out into the wilderness, where the Devil tempted him for forty days. He ate nothing all that time and was very hungry.

Then the Devil said to him, 'If you are the Son of God, change this stone into a loaf of bread.' But Jesus told him, 'No! The Scriptures say, "People need more than bread for their life.'"

Then the Devil took him up and revealed to him all the kingdoms of the world in a moment of time. The Devil told him, 'I will give you the glory of these kingdoms and authority over them–because they are mine to give to anyone I please. I will give it all to you if you will bow down and worship me.'

Jesus replied, 'The Scriptures, say, "You must worship the Lord your God; serve only him.'"

Then the Devil took him to Jerusalem, to the highest point of the Temple, and said, 'If you are the Son of God, jump off! For the Scriptures say, "He orders his angels to protect and guard you. And they will hold you with their hands to keep you from striking your foot on a stone.' "

Jesus responded, 'The Scriptures also say, "Do not test the Lord your God.' "

When the Devil had finished tempting Jesus, he left him until the next opportunity came."

Sometimes, I think we don't realize how the Devil is so deceiving...after all, he is the father of all lies. He quotes scripture and he comes to us when we don't think he will bother us. Jesus had just finished a very important part of God's plan for his life. He was "riding the crest of the wave," and didn't expect to be tempted at this moment. Isn't that exactly how it is for us? Jesus did not yield and he never sinned...but we often fall into the trap of being deceived and we sin. I am so grateful we can confess our sins and be totally restored to fellowship with our Heavenly Father.

Jesus was full of the Spirit...and the temptation came. Temptation relates to the areas of our lives where we are most vulnerable. The lust of the eye, the pride of life, nothing new. We are all tempted by our own desires and when we disobey we have to confess and repent.

1 John 5:18-21
"We know that those who have become part of God's family do not make a practice of sinning, for God's Son holds them securely, and the evil one cannot get his hands on them. We know that we are children of God and that the world around us is under the power and control of the evil one. And we know that the Son of God has come, and he has given us understanding so that we can know the true God. And now we are in God because we are in his Son, Jesus Christ. He is the only true God, and he is eternal life.

Dear children, keep away from anything that might take God's place in your hearts."

When we understand these scriptures and we start to apply it to our hearts we are finally walking in step with the Spirit. We know we have someone we can go to with all of our temptations and He will and does provide a way of escape.

Jesus was tempted in all ways as we are tempted...but He was without sin. He understands our temptations and He has compassion for us and will provide the Holy Spirit to help us through those times of being drawn away into sin.

I cannot relate to what Jesus went through...and I cannot evaluate what the children of Israel experienced for forty years. I can read it, and I understand it was because of rebellion and disobedience...but I do not know how they lived it. It is a challenge to me when I read the Scriptures and I ask God to help me not to fall into unhealthy patterns of thinking and living. It keeps me thinking in terms of what temptation and sin does when I allow it to reign in my heart over a period of time without confession and repentance.

Hebrews 3:8-13

"Don't harden your hearts against him as Israel did when they rebelled, when they tested God's patience in the wilderness. There your ancestors tried my patience, even though they saw my miracles for forty years. So I was angry with them, and I said, 'Their hearts always turn away from me. They refuse to do what I tell them.' So in my anger I made a vow: 'They will never enter my place of rest.'

Be careful then, dear friends. Make sure that your own hearts are not evil and unbelieving, turning you away from the living God. You must warn each other every day, as long as it is called 'today,' so that none of you will be deceived by sin and hardened against God."

Forty Days...or Forty Years...either one is not something I would want to experience, ever. My Mom had a little saying about sin and temptation, "The birds might fly through your hair, but don't let them build a nest." I realize Martin Luther said it first, but coming from my Mother it had more meaning. One day at a time...and learning to give our times to the Lord is the beginning of wisdom.

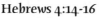

Hebrews 4:14-16

"That is why we have a great High Priest who has gone to heaven, Jesus the Son of God. Let us cling to him and never stop trusting him. This High Priest of ours understands our weaknesses, for he faced all of the same temptations we do, yet he did not sin. So let us come boldly to the throne of our gracious God. There we will receive his mercy, and we will find grace to help us when we need it."

As you journal today think about the potential times in your life when you will be faced with temptations. Ask Him to guide you and help you during those times.

Hebrews 10:21-24

"And since we have a great High Priest who rules over God's people, let us go right into the presence of God, with true hearts fully trusting him. For our evil consciences have been sprinkled with Christ's blood to make us clean, and our bodies have been washed with pure water.

Without wavering, let us hold tightly to the hope we say we have, for God can be trusted to keep his promise. Think of ways to encourage one another to outbursts of love and good deeds."

We are free from the curse of sin...therefore, let us go forth rejoicing and caring for one another.

Journaling today should consist of confession, repentance, and freedom. Learning to keep in step with the Spirit and walking in freedom as forgiven people is so uplifting...and it brings praise to our Heavenly Father!

My Daily Journal

DAY

34

DAY 35

Wait for your turn!

When I was a child attending grade school, I was among those who were small. If we were being lined up according to size, I would be first...which was a good thing...but if it was first come, first served you can imagine. I seldom found myself among those to be first in line. Often when I was close to the front and the teacher was not around the bigger girls would push me aside and get in line ahead of me...if you have never been short...*there, I said it*...you probably won't even get this modern day parable. I was many times forced to go to the end of the line. This made an impression on me...because it was not about being first...it was about who was the strongest or the biggest.

> **Proverbs 25:6-7**
> "Don't demand an audience with the king or push for a place among the great. It is better to wait for an invitation than to be sent to the end of the line, publicly disgraced!"

> **Proverbs 25:27**
> "Just as it is not good to eat too much honey, it is not good for people to think about all the honors they deserve."

I learned as I grew older that the true heart of a leader was a person who was also a servant. It was about putting others first and serving rather than being served. It was a concept so different from what the world teaches and how the world values people who serve. "Getting Ahead," in this world means you have to be strong and you have to be first...but not so when it comes to building the Kingdom.

> **Matthew 20:20-28**
> "Then the mother of James and John, the sons of Zebedee, came to Jesus with her sons. She knelt respectfully to ask a favor. 'What is your request?' he asked.
>
> She replied, 'In your Kingdom, will you let my two sons sit in places of honor next to you, one at your right and the other at your left?'

But Jesus told them, 'You don't know what you are asking! Are you able to drink from the bitter cup of sorrow I am about to drink?'

'Oh yes,' they replied, 'we are able!'

'You will indeed drink from it,' he told them. 'But I have no right to say who will sit on the thrones next to mine. My Father has prepared those places for the ones he has chosen.'

When the ten other disciples heard what James and John had asked, they were indignant. But Jesus called them together and said, 'You know that in this world kings are tyrants, and officials lord it over the people beneath them. But among you it should be quite different. Whoever wants to be a leader among you must be your servant, and whoever wants to be first must become your slave. For even I, the Son of Man, came here not to be served but to serve others, and to give my life as a ransom for many.'"

Waiting for our turn takes on a totally new concept...it means waiting upon others. Allowing others to be first. I love to see the body of Christ practicing this truth.

We were standing in line for our food at our Singles Retreat...one of the men in our group suggested we allow the speaker and his wife to go first...I thought it was truly a good thing. There are times when we need to honor others better than ourselves and honor them for their work's sake. It was a good feeling. The speaker, was my son and his wife. How fun for me to observe and see the kindness of the group practicing this principal. I watch our new members come into our group broken and sometimes very wounded...our group as a body cares for them...and they receive and then they pass it on.

Jesus washed the feet of the disciples...he took upon Himself the role of a servant and washed their feet. How humbling for the disciples and what an example of the master.

We need to serve one another with our gifts and build one another up by sharing our gifts in whatever way we have opportunity. Our gifts have been given to us for the purpose of building up the body of Christ...not for our own purposes.

Matthew 16:25
"If you try to keep your life for yourself, you will lose it. But if you give up your life for me, you will find true life."

166

The teaching of a secular world isn't about waiting upon others...or serving others...it is about being in charge and getting ahead so others can serve you. It is difficult to help children learn to be patient and wait...even sharing with others. Little two-year-olds have a favorite expression, "It is mine!" We have to learn as wise parents to encourage them with the teaching of it is not always about them and having all of their needs met, or they will grow up with thinking it is all about them. We have neglected teaching them the wisdom of God and allowed them to think they are the center of the universe. This self-serving philosophy is not very attractive in the adult world. Little children grow up and need to care and share. If we don't teach them about God's plan, we can end up caring for them all of their lives...and if they marry...their partner will have to assume your role in their lives.

We cannot always be first...we have to learn to wait for our turn.

Philippians 2:5-11
"Your attitude should be the same that Christ Jesus had. Though he was God, he did not demand and cling to his rights as God. He made himself nothing; he took the humble position of a slave and appeared in human form. And in human form he obediently humbled himself even further by dying a criminal's death on a cross. Because of this, God raised him up to the heights of heaven and gave him the name that is above every other name, so that at the name of Jesus every knee will bow, in heaven and on earth and under the earth, and every tongue will confess that Jesus Christ is Lord, to the glory of God the Father."

Journaling should be starting to feel very important in your life. Thinking and writing about what you are learning and then seeing how God is challenging you to apply it in your life can be very satisfying to you personally. We know it is important when we learn a truth...and then apply it to our daily lives.

My Daily
Journal

DAY
35

Don't go until you receive what the Father has promised!

DAY 36

I sometimes wonder what it must have felt like for the disciples after the Lord returned to His Father. They seemingly were thrust out there to do ministry and left to the wolves. It might have appeared that way to some...but we know better. They were being asked to do what they were called to do...Serve and Reach others.

I remember the first time I was asked to teach a simple flannel graph lesson for boys and girls. It was a Friday afternoon five day club and it was scary. Little children sitting on the floor looking up with an expectation and I was the teacher. It all seems so many years ago. I was only thirteen and it was the beginning of a plan God had for my life...being a teacher of the word of God was a very high calling but it felt so lonely on that day so long ago. Mrs. Null, just stood in the background and watched. Her student became a teacher and a helper.

The Disciples had been given a command...

Matthew 28:16-20
"Then the eleven disciples left for Galilee, going to the mountain where Jesus had told them to go. When they saw him, they worshiped him–but some of them still doubted!

Jesus came and told his disciples, 'I have been given complete authority in heaven and on earth. Therefore, go and make disciples of all the nations, baptizing them in the name of the Father and the Son and the Holy Spirit. Teach these new disciples to obey all the commands I have given you. And be sure of this; I am with you always, even to the end of the age.' "

Acts 1:4-5
"In one of these meetings as he was eating a meal with them, he told them, 'Do not leave Jerusalem until the Father sends you what he promised. Remember, I have told you about this before. John baptized with water, but in just a few days you will be baptized with the Holy Spirit.' "

Now they were waiting in Jerusalem...for what had been promised.

169

There is a commercial that says, "Don't leave home without it!" It was very important for the disciples not to move forward without the power of the Holy Spirit. We can do nothing aside from the inspiration of the Holy Spirit...the One who empowers us when we are doing service for the King. All authority has been given to us...when we do His bidding in *His name and in the power of the Holy Spirit.*

Acts 2: 1-4
"On the day of Pentecost, seven weeks after Jesus' resurrection, the believers were meeting together in one place. Suddenly, there was a sound from heaven like the roaring of a mighty wind storm in the skies above them, and it filled the house where they were meeting. Then, what looked like flames or tongues of fire appeared and settled on each of them. And everyone present was filled with the Holy Spirit and began speaking in other languages, as the Holy Spirit gave them this ability."

I cannot imagine what this must have been like for the disciples. I have thought about this event and wondered...what kinds of thoughts must have been going on in their minds. The people who were there to observe thought they might be drunk. People from other nations understood what was being said in their own native language.

Acts 2:12-13
"They stood there amazed and perplexed. 'What can this mean?' they asked each other. But others in the crowd were mocking. 'They're drunk, that's all!' they said."

Have you ever encountered a time in your life when you knew without the power of the Holy Spirit working in your life you were, "busted." We attempt to serve God so often without waiting for Him to lead us, guide us, and fill us for the mission He has called us to do. We can do nothing in our own strength. We get tired of waiting sometimes and run ahead of God's leading in our lives and the waiting becomes more than what we are able to handle and we fall flat on our faces. It is a humbling experience and if you learn it early in life you never forget why you need to wait for His leading and direction and filling in your life.

Sometimes, I read my notes before I am getting ready to do a retreat and they look dead and useless and just plain flat. They are, when they are just my words...but when the anointing of the Holy Spirit comes, the words become His words and they are powerful and have validation. It is truly amazing.

In the ordinary things we do in our lives, we need to wait for the empowering of the Holy Spirit. We need to seek His counsel and guidance daily, otherwise, we are walking in our own strength and it is not a good thing. We cannot build the Kingdom in our own strength.

Acts 2:14-16

"Then Peter stepped forward with the eleven other apostles and shouted to the crowd, 'Listen carefully, all of you, fellow Jews and residents of Jerusalem! Make no mistake about this. Some of you are saying these people are drunk. It isn't true! It's much too early for that. People don't get drunk by nine o'clock in the morning. No, what you see this morning was predicted centuries ago by the prophet Joel.'"

Peter preached a powerful message on that day...

Acts 2:43-47

"A deep sense of awe came over them all, and the apostles performed many miraculous signs and wonders. And all the believers met together constantly and shared everything they had. They sold their possessions and shared the proceeds with those in need. They worshiped together at the Temple each day, met in homes for the Lord's Supper, and shared their meals with great joy and generosity–all the while praising God and enjoying the goodwill of all the people. And each day the Lord added to their group those who were being saved."

They waited for the Holy Spirit to fill them for service and many good things happened. I know the difference He makes in my life when I am doing something in my own strength and what it looks like when I am doing it in the strength that God provides. I have wanted to run ahead of the Lord many times...because I want things to get done within my time frame...*how silly is that for crying out loud!*

We have to learn to wait upon the Lord. For some of us, learning about how weak we are without Him is the only way we learn this truth.

We can't take the show on the road without the Holy Spirit!

All through the book of Acts we see the many great things the Apostles did as the Holy Spirit filled them with boldness for service.

Acts 4:31
"After this prayer, the building where they were meeting shook, and they were all filled with the Holy Spirit. And they preached God's message with boldness."

Journaling today is about asking you to consider what it means to be filled with the Holy Spirit...and being filled with Him for service...sharing the gospel message calls for holy boldness and power.

It is the same today as it was in the days when Peter and the others walked through the streets of Jerusalem...in the book of Acts.

My Daily
Journal

DAY

36

DAY 37

You're too late... Our brother is already dead!

The sisters had cared for their brother and were totally devoted. They were a household of single people living together in community. It doesn't say in the scriptures, exactly what their circumstances were but maybe their parents had died early and the children remained in the home. They were all single and not married and they were friends with Jesus. Now there brother was dead!

John 11:17-29
"When Jesus arrived at Bethany, he was told that Lazarus had already been in his grave for four days. Bethany was only a few miles down the road from Jerusalem, and many of the people had come to pay their respects and console Martha and Mary on their loss. When Martha got word that Jesus was coming, she went to meet him. But Mary stayed at home. Martha said to Jesus, 'Lord, if you had been here, my brother would not have died. But even now I know that God will give you whatever you ask.'

Jesus told her, 'Your brother will rise again.'

'Yes,' Martha said, 'when everyone else rises, on resurrection day.'

Jesus told her, 'I am the resurrection and the life. Those who believe in me, even though they die like everyone else, will live again. They are given eternal life for believing in me and will never perish. Do you believe this, Martha?'

'Yes, Lord,' she told him. 'I have always believed you are the Messiah, the Son of God, the one who has come into the world from God.' Then she left him and returned to Mary. She called Mary aside from the mourners and told her, 'The Teacher is here and wants to see you.' So Mary immediately went to him."

It was truly a miracle. Jesus raised Lazarus from the dead! His life was returned to him on that day and it was a turning point in the life of Christ.

It was the final straw for the Pharisees and they immediately started to set in motion the plot to get rid of this man' Jesus...who was becoming more and more popular every day. He was not someone they could quickly dismiss, he was someone to be reckoned with and they seemingly could not understand his authority or the power he seemed to possess which gave authority and power.

Did you ever think about why Jesus waited so long to go see Lazarus? Thomas questioned that as well.

John 11:14
"Then he told them plainly, 'Lazarus is dead. And for your sake, I am glad I wasn't there, because this will give you another opportunity to believe in me. Come, let's go see him.'"

The disciples were still being taught lessons in faith building. Simple messages for them from Jesus. They would need to remember these times as they began the ministry without the physical presence of Jesus. His Spirit would be with them...and the Holy Spirit would be leading and directing them as they preached, healed, and cast out demons. They would look back and remember all of these visual aids Jesus left in their memory banks which would give them courage and hope.

Timing is everything. We have talked about this concept a lot in this little book of Daily Journals. We have reminded ourselves over and over again that God is never late...and His timing is always when it needs to be. It is a learning process for us...believing God and learning to trust His wisdom deepens our walk with Him and gives us courage to step out by faith. When we think in terms of God's timing and His Purpose and Plan we realize just how awesome He really is, and we are able to give Glory to His Name. It is once again, a matter of learning the truth of the statement, God is in charge. He is God and I'm not!

Recently we moved the clocks back and the fall days became even shorter. It seemed like in one week we were in the throws of winter. I laughed to myself...winter indeed...after all, I wasn't living in Minnesota and winter was only a few short months rather than 6 months of cold harsh below zero temperatures and snow covered roads. The memories are still in my mind...but the reality of living where I live had to be clearly challenged.

One hour had caused a whole lot of negative thinking to go on in my head. My little world had been rocked by one hour. I needed a reality check...for sure!

We want God to hurry up and take care of a situation. We want the weather to fit our clothes. We want the days to be longer...and we all want to live where everything goes our way. I believe Dorothy was looking for a place called Oz, where life would always be as she liked. But she finally ended up in Kansas after all.

God has a purpose in our lives, but it is difficult sometimes to be on the same page with God's thinking. We want it *our way and on our terms.* I admire Martha, she knew the truth, and even though her brother was dead she knew if Jesus asked the Father...the situation could change. Isn't that the biggest faith statement EVER!

As you Journal today ask God to increase your faith. To build you up in the matter of living by faith and not by sight. The light hasn't gone away...it just gets darker an hour earlier. Even when situations seem really bad...we need to focus on what is really going on...and what is really happening. If you are facing a difficult time now...ask God to reveal His power in your life. Pray for others who are experiencing low times. Our purpose and meaning is found in Him!

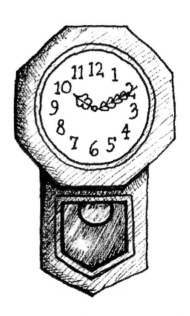

My Daily Journal

DAY
37

DAY 38

Truth stands the test of time

Some people are as good as their word! I remember as a child people would give you their word and it was as binding as a legal contract. A person was known by their word...what they promised they would do. They lived up to their commitments and if at all humanly possible, they would do what they had agreed to do.

Proverbs 12:19
"Truth stands the test of time; lies are soon exposed."

No one wants to be exposed as a liar. No one wants to be caught up in a lie. We desire for truth to be the foundation of who we are...but we know lies have always been a part of who we are from time to time. Are we not grateful for the mercy and grace of God? I surely am.

My Mother would tell me as a child, "Tell me the truth and it will be better for you than if you tell me a lie." She made a believer out of me. Sometimes the truth is painful, it causes us pain and others pain. I learned a huge lesson when I learned the concept of being set free, and the truth of being set free has lasted me a life time. *It was almost too good to be true...but it was true.*

John 14:6
"Jesus told him, 'I am the way, the truth, and the life. No man can come to the Father except through me.'"

Jesus was having this conversation with the Jewish religious leaders of his day. They were unhappy with people saying that Jesus was the Son of God. They were unhappy with a lot of things about Jesus...his healing people on the sabbath, hanging out with sinners and lepers. Jesus was very wise and always knew what they were thinking. He had this little conversation with some of them. It is very interesting to note how God speaks truth in this passage.

John 8:31-47
"Jesus said to the people who believed in him, 'You are truly my disciples if you keep obeying my teachings. And you will know the truth, and the truth will set you free.'

'But we are descendants of Abraham,' they said. 'We have never been slaves to anyone on earth. What do you mean, "set free?"'

Jesus replied, 'I assure you that everyone who sins is a slave of sin. A slave is not a permanent member of the family, but a son is part of the family forever. So if the Son sets you free, you will indeed be free. Yes, I realize that you are descendants of Abraham. And yet some of you are trying to kill me because my message does not find a place in your hearts. I am telling you what I saw when I was with my Father. But you are following the advice of your father.'

'Our father is Abraham,' they declared.

'No,' Jesus replied, 'for if you were children of Abraham, you would follow his good example. I told you the truth I heard from God, you are trying to kill me. Abraham wouldn't do a thing like that. No, you are obeying your real father when you act that way.'

They replied, 'We were not born out of wedlock! Our true Father is God himself.'

Jesus told them, 'If God were your Father, you would love me, because I have come to you from God. I am not here on my own, but he sent me. Why can't you understand what I am saying? It is because you are unable to do so! For you are the children of your father the Devil, and you love to do the evil things he does. He was a murderer from the beginning and has always hated the truth. There is no truth in him. When he lies, it is consistent with his character; for he is a liar and the father of lies. So when I tell the truth, you just naturally don't believe me! Which of you can truthfully accuse me of sin? And since I am telling you the truth, why don't you believe me? Anyone whose Father is God listens gladly to the words of God. Since you don't, it proves you aren't God's children.'"

This is such a powerful portion of scripture. When I read it, I feel convicted and ashamed. I know I fall short of what God's expectations are for me. I do not know how any of us could be or do anything without totally understanding the mercy and grace of God. We keep falling short of God's expectations...and He keeps providing mercy and grace for us because in spite of missing the mark, He absolutely still loves us. It is not about our ability to be good and faithful, it is about His faithfulness and His mercy!

We would be unable to stand with the scrutiny of God in our face!

We would be forever condemned...but enter the grace and mercy of God, His truth has indeed set us free from the bondage of sin and the curse of sin.

Romans 6:12-14

"Do not let sin control the way you live; do not give in to its lustful desires. Do not let any part of your body become a tool of wickedness, to be used for sinning. Instead, give yourselves completely to God since you have been given new life. And use your whole body as a tool to do what is right for the glory of God. Sin is no longer your master, for you are no longer subject to the law, which enslaves you to sin. Instead, you are free by God's grace."

I am so glad I "understand the meaning of truth in every sense of the word." The truth has indeed set us free.

Romans 3:21-24

"But now God has shown us a different way of being right in his sight–not by obeying the law but by the way promised in the Scriptures long ago. We are made right in God's sight when we trust in Jesus Christ to take away our sins. And we all can be saved in this same way, no matter who we are or what we have done.

For all have sinned; all fall short of God's glorious standard. Yet now God in his gracious kindness declares us not guilty. He has done this through Christ Jesus, who has freed us by taking away our sins."

What a blessing! What freedom...finally realizing that no matter what we are guilty of, we can finally believe His truth stands the test of time. If we know the truth and have accepted the truth into our lives...we have eternal life.

Psalm 95:9-11

"For there your ancestors tried my patience; they courted my wrath though they had seen my many miracles.

For forty years I was angry with them, and I said, 'They are a people whose hearts turn away from me. They refuse to do what I tell them.'

So in my anger I made a vow: 'They will never enter my place of rest.'"

Those in the wilderness fell and were never allowed into the promised land. They believed a lie...they refused to trust the truth and follow Moses and turn to God in times of testing and troubles. I pray we learn the lesson of listening to the truth and obedience is our course. It is the only way..."Trust and Obey, for there is no other way, to be happy in Jesus, but to Trust and Obey."

Confess today your sins and live in the freedom of the truth. Journal your thoughts today on the topic of walking in the freedom of the Spirit.

My Daily Journal

DAY

38

Hurry up! The rain is coming!

DAY 39

Have you ever been caught in a fast approaching rain storm? Suddenly a rain shower appears and you are caught in it with no umbrella, just out there. Sometimes, we see the clouds...dark and foreboding...but for some reason we think we can beat the rain and make it home.

Does the announcement of oncoming destruction in our path cause us to change our patterns or hurry us along to where we finally make a wiser choice? Sometimes! But for the most part, we tend to believe we will escape somehow and not get caught! We don't actually base our lives upon the possible reality of how bad things happen to good people...we might if we are living in depression, because then we think everything that is going to happen to us will be bad. I don't think we should go around looking for doom and gloom either but planning ahead doesn't hurt either. Making wise choices can be a factor in what's up ahead!

My house looks pretty clean on cloudy days...but when the clouds disappear because of the sunlight...look out! The windows are dirty, the dust is everywhere. I have to make some quick choices. I have to dust and clean and sweep...but I never really find the time to get to the windows...funny how that works! My personal life needs the exposure of the Son, as well...probably more than I care to admit.

Ephesians four, talks about how we should live as children of the Light... there are some challenges there to renew our thoughts and attitudes.

Ephesians 4:24
"You must display a new nature because you are a new person, created in God's likeness–righteous, holy, and true."

Ephesians 4:31-32
"Get rid of all bitterness, rage, anger, harsh words, and slander, as well as all types of malicious behavior. Instead, be kind to each other, tenderhearted, forgiving one another, just as God through Christ has forgiven you."

A few cobwebs revealed in those verses!

This kind of challenge is warning us...we may be walking in the light at one moment but without the Holy Spirit living in and through us. *We are still going to have to deal with those rainy days...and we need to be prepared before the darkness overtakes us and we camouflage the sin.* If we are caught in the rain...we are covered by the Spirit of God and He will protect us. He becomes our umbrella. We are reminded to guard our hearts. Be Prepared!

> **Proverbs 4:23**
> "Above all else, guard your heart, for it affects everything you do."

Rainy days do have an affect upon our attitudes. We just had a period of seven days of rain, clouds, and no sunshine. Everyone was down in the mouth...out comes the sun...and the world was a better place. It is true. The enemy will use whatever it takes to deceive, discourage and cause you to doubt what is going on in our lives, but he is not in control...no indeed, not in any way, shape or form. He wants to get us distracted and off the path. He wants to disrupt our faith walk and have us think we have to walk by sight. I know...I have been there! I must discipline my life to walk in His light and in His Glory. We all do!

> **Proverbs 3:7-8**
> "Don't be impressed with your own wisdom. Instead, fear the LORD and turn your back on evil. Then you will gain renewed health and vitality."

> **Proverbs 3:21-26**
> "My child, don't lose sight of good planning and insight. Hang on to them, for they fill you with life and bring you honor and respect. They keep you safe on your way and keep your feet from stumbling. You can lie down without fear and enjoy pleasant dreams. You need not be afraid of disaster or the destruction that comes upon the wicked, for the LORD is your security. He will keep your foot from being caught in a trap."

When we see the clouds, we need to grab our umbrellas...which is our covering...the Holy Spirit. He is the one who will give us wisdom and protect and counsel us in all situations. Whatever we are facing we are covered! I am totally dependent upon Him to guide and direct me.

I know the other side of the coin says, "There shall be showers of Blessing." This is a promise. I was using the rain as a metaphor to describe a negative...but we can see the rain as a blessing as well. My Mom always reminds me, "The rain falls on the just and the unjust!" We laugh about her statement, because she will call and ask me if it is raining on the unjust...referring to me and my house. We just laugh. We only live four blocks apart...so how does that figure!

We read in the New Testament about the rains coming down and the floods coming up and the house on the sand falling flat. In the Old Testament, the rain destroyed the earth in the during the days of Noah...and then God gave the promise of the rainbow to remind the people that he would never destroy the earth again by a flood. Elijah prayed and it did not rain for three years and then he prayed again and it rained.

1 Kings 18:1-2
"After many months passed, in the third year of the drought, the LORD said to Elijah, 'Go and present yourself to King Ahab. Tell him that I will soon send rain!' So Elijah went to appear before Ahab."

1 Kings 18:41-46
"Then Elijah said to Ahab, 'Go and enjoy a good meal! For I hear a mighty rainstorm coming!'

So Ahab prepared a feast. But Elijah climbed to the top of Mount Carmel and fell to the ground and prayed. Then he said to his servant, 'Go and look out toward the sea.'

The servant went and looked, but he returned to Elijah and said, 'I didn't see anything.' Seven times Elijah told him to go and look, and seven times he went. Finally the seventh time, his servant told him, 'I saw a little cloud about the size of a hand rising from the sea.'

Then Elijah shouted, 'Hurry to Ahab and tell him, "Climb into your chariot and go back home. If you don't hurry, the rain will stop you!"'

And sure enough, the sky was soon black with clouds. A heavy wind brought a terrific rainstorm, and Ahab left quickly for Jezreel. Now the LORD gave special strength to Elijah. He tucked his cloak into his belt and ran ahead of Ahab's chariot all the way to the entrance of Jezreel."

We really don't know the power of faith and prayer. God is able to break through the normal things we see in life. He is the ruler of heaven and earth. Jesus spoke to the waves in the midst of a powerful storm and said, "Peace be still." The wind stopped and the waves subsided and the water was peaceful.

He is the Ruler of Everything!

When I think of the phrase, "Hurry, the rain is coming," I always think of this account in scripture of a prophet's prayer and a God who can do anything...what a Mighty God we serve! As you journal today think of some situations in your life where God has taken you beyond the normal and blessed your life in a great and mighty way...or ask Him to reveal His power in your life so you may get a glimpse of His presence.

My Daily Journal

DAY

39

I've been waiting but nothing is happening

DAY 40

Sometimes I feel like the world is passing me by and nothing is going on that is very exciting or newsworthy. I am sure it is just me, because I know that every day is a gift of time. The Lord says every day is a gift. I know it, but when we live life expecting something to happen we often miss what is happening. Living in the present requires discipline and taking a real look at the reality of what God is doing on a daily basis.

Our lives are very busy and sometimes we miss out on the true meaning of the day.

Psalm 8:3-9
"When I look at the night sky and see the work of your fingers–the moon and the stars you have set in place–what are mortals that you should think of us, mere humans that you should care for us? For you made us only a little lower than God, and you crowned us with glory and honor. You put us in charge of everything you made, giving us authority over all things–the sheep and the cattle and all the wild animals, the birds in the sky, the fish in the sea, and everything that swims the ocean currents."

We have a lot going on as we enjoy life and live each day to the fullest.

Psalm 46:1
"God is our refuge and strength, always ready to help in times of trouble."

Some days seem full of trouble and we just don't know what will happen...but it is a comfort to know and realize that in spite of everything...God is in control. We are His!

Psalm 146:8b
"The LORD lifts the burdens of those bent beneath their loads."

Ecclesiastes 1:3-11
"What do people get for all their hard work? Generations come

and go, but nothing really changes. The sun rises and sets and hurries around to rise again. The wind blows south and north, here and there, twisting back and forth, getting nowhere. The rivers run into the sea, but the sea is never full. Then the water returns again to the rivers and flows again to the sea. Everything is so weary and tiresome! No matter how much we see, we are never satisfied. No matter how much we hear, we are not content.

History merely repeats itself. It has all been done before. Nothing under the sun is truly new. What can you point to that is new? How do you know it didn't already exist long ago? We don't remember what happened in those former times. And in future generations, no one will remember what we are doing now."

If we just looked at our world without the hope of Jesus Christ in our lives, it would indeed seem meaningless. But our lives have meaning and purpose and we know that God is watching over us and caring about us and He has a personal interest in each one of us. Our lives may seem like we are just hanging out and waiting for something to happen...but God really does care about what we are doing and what is happening in our lives. I am so thankful to know that from God's word.

He cares about us...and our problems and burdens are known to Him!

1 Peter 5:7
"Give all your worries and cares to God, for he cares about what happens to you."

He cares for us...and He helps us to care for others. We are God's care packages to one another. He shows His care to us personally and He sends the body of Christ to care for us as well.

1 Peter 4:11b
"Are you called to help others? Do it with all the strength and energy that God supplies. Then God will be given glory in everything through Jesus Christ. All glory and power belong to him forever and ever. Amen"

1 Peter 2:5
"And now God is building you, as living stones, into his spiritual temple. What's more, you are God's holy priests, who offer the spiritual sacrifices that please him because of Jesus Christ."

We are representing Him daily...offering the sacrifices of praise that

188

bring honor and glory to His name. I don't think about this one too much...it is beyond my thinking at times.

He tells us in 1 Peter we are chosen. He has called us out of darkness into His wonderful light...we have a mission and a purpose. We are chosen, how wonderful...chosen for service!

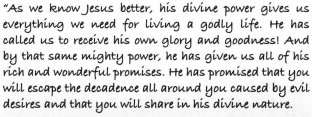

2 Peter 1:3-11

"As we know Jesus better, his divine power gives us everything we need for living a godly life. He has called us to receive his own glory and goodness! And by that same mighty power, he has given us all of his rich and wonderful promises. He has promised that you will escape the decadence all around you caused by evil desires and that you will share in his divine nature.

So make every effort to apply the benefits of these promises to your life. Then your faith will produce a life of moral excellence. A life of moral excellence leads to knowing God better. Knowing God leads to self-control. Self-control leads to patient endurance, and patient endurance leads to godliness. Godliness leads to love for other Christians, and finally you will grow to have genuine love for everyone. The more you grow like this, the more you will become productive and useful in your knowledge of our Lord Jesus Christ. But those who fail to develop these virtues are blind or, at least, very shortsighted. They have already forgotten that God has cleansed them from their old life of sin.

So, dear friends, work hard to prove that you really are among those God has called and chosen. Doing this, you will never stumble or fall away. And God will open wide the gates of heaven for you to enter into the eternal Kingdom of our Lord and Savior Jesus Christ."

These verses have been for years a guideline for what it means to live daily productive lives. I am not just living my life waiting for something to happen...I am living my life and **God is allowing** all kinds of wonderful things to happen. I can either participate and be part of what He is doing or I can choose not to be involved. If I want to have a full and meaningful life I can be a participant. I can stand up and be counted.

"The more you grow like this, the more you will become productive and useful in your knowledge of our Lord Jesus Christ."

For myself, this is the true meaning of life...being productive and useful growing in my knowledge of Christ.

I Choose to Participate!

What counts for you? Journal from your heart. We have been on a forty day journey, I am not sure where you have been...or where you are going. But for me, I am taking it...one day at a time. Sweet Jesus, I am choosing to grow with the Lord...each and every day by His Grace.

My Daily Journal

DAY 40